Meet Mr and Mrs Smith

Undercover Legends

David Le Courageux

Hendry Publishing

Contents

1. Introduction   1

2. Prologue   3

3. Chapter 1   5
   Money Laundering

4. Chapter 2   11
   What Makes Them Tick?

5. Chapter 3   14
   Samantha Session One

6. Chapter 4   21
   Samantha Session Two

7. Chapter 5   29
   Dominic Session One

8. Chapter 6   35
   Dominic Session Two

9. Chapter 7   42
   Dominic Session Three

10. Chapter 8   44
    Dominic Session Four

11. Chapter 9   53
    Dominic Session Five

12. Chapter 10   55
    Dominic Session Six

13. Chapter 11   62
    Dominic Session Seven

14. Chapter 12   70
    Dominic Session Eight

15. Chapter 13   74
    Paul Nuemann

16. Author's Note   76

About the Author   78

Also By   80

Introduction

THE UNDERCOVER POLICE OFFICERS (UCOs) Dominic and Samantha Smith are the Mr and Mrs Smith you are about to meet. Dom and Sam as they are known to each other and many more.

You know it's not unusual for couples, married or not, to engage in the same profession or do the same job. Richard and Judy sit in the same studio and talk into a camera for a living. Enough of them. Mr and Mrs Smith may one day be interviewed by R and J. That would be weird. The studio would have to be darkened so no one can see the faces of the two former undercover officers. You may suggest they cover their heads in blood-soaked sheets and have a cameraman spray luminol. Then you would at least see two ectoplasms... some goo glowing in the dark. Not nice at all. The other couple that springs to mind are Bill and Hilary. Surely, they were both Presidents? Oops... no, Bill was, and Hilary was a wannabe.

You possibly know doctors, lawyers, accountants, even librarians who are a couple. But odds on, you don't know of a couple who were undercover officers until now. These are their stories. Sometimes as individuals. Sometimes as a couple. Sometimes involving courage. Sometimes hilarious and sometimes sad. Always using stealth and tradecraft when infiltrating organised crime groups. The story that follows is based on true events and real people.

We ask the reader to note that any undercover officer has a front and backstage existence, a bit like an actor. The front is on the stage performing a role. Backstage is partly his or her private life and in part the support and backup from the cover officers and the team. Those parts are the life support system enabling the actors' performances.

This book, an introduction to the Undercover Legends series , should be seen as a primer or a 101 to the world of covert policing in the United Kingdom in the 21st century.

Prologue

"IT'S WRITTEN IN THE stars," someone, somewhere once said. Dominic and Samantha Smith became two comets in the undercover universe. For many years, they burned brightly, separately carving out successful careers as elite undercover cops until they collided. And, what a collision! Rather than be destroyed in the inferno, eventually they fused into a fearsome partnership within a formidable undercover deployment known as Operation Candle.

Together, Dom and Sam became stronger. Both would scoff at any notion they were romantics, but their story is a romance even if it was partly born out of pragmatism. They became partners in life as well as undercover partners. They also became the guardians of an extended family that included Sam's son, James, and Dom's children from his two previous marriages, H and BB from his second marriage, and Jane and Lesley from his first marriage. Dom always had a close and supportive relationship with all four of his children. They grew up as brothers and sisters minus the prefix 'step.'

James also became part of the Smith family as did his birth father, Ken, in a way. Sam and Ken were divorced amicably after a few years of marriage when they were still young. Sam knew it happened because she was determined to succeed in her career as a police officer. She was another statistic in the high divorce rate amongst career police officers, particularly detectives. Now divorced, she was resolved to forge ahead in her police career as a single mum. That wasn't easy as misogyny was common in the police service. With the help of Ken and her parents, Sam was able to arrange childcare to pursue her goals in a demanding environment.

Sam checked off those goals. First, she was a CID detective. Then she worked on major crime investigation units until she decided she wanted to become an undercover police officer, a UCO. At first, her line manager tried to tell her she wouldn't make it as she was a single mother. Undeterred and in typical Sam-style, she bypassed this misogynist's nonsense and went straight to the very top – the Assistant Chief Constable (Crime) in her force. He approved her application and eventually she got there after passing the tough National Undercover Accreditation Course (NUTAC) some years after Dom had taken a similar career path. Their stars were now aligned but their trajectories didn't cross until Dom needed a female UCO for Operation Candle.

At the early stages of Operation Candle, and whilst Dom was putting together his team, he heard about Sam's role in the money laundering operation. She had made her mark in the world of elite undercover policing.

Chapter 1

Money Laundering

THE DEPLOYMENT ON THE money laundering job brought Sam to the attention of those who matter in the world of undercover policing. In time, she would also come to Dom's attention when he recruited her for his Operation Candle team. Life as a police officer wasn't always that straightforward for her. Sam had been a police cadet, then at nineteen became a regular copper. At twenty, she became pregnant with James and married his father, Ken. On returning to work Sam concentrated on her career, rapidly progressing to the CID as a detective. That focus cost her marriage, for when she was twenty-three Ken and Sam amicably separated. Ken later remarried but he and his new wife were still part of an extended family for James as they provided childcare when Sam's mum and dad were not available.

Sam, now a single mum, progressed from regular CID work to becoming a Test Purchase Officer, a TPO, involved in street-level drugs buys. This was a steppingstone to undercover work once she had successfully passed the National Undercover Training Accreditation Course, NUTAC. By the time she gave evidence in the money laundering trial, Sam was the real deal: an elite undercover police officer.

Every inch of her svelte five feet-nine inches, looking like a wealthy and successful Independent Financial Advisor, an IFA, Sam walked into the number one court at the Old Bailey from a door behind the judge's bench. Well, why wouldn't she? Unlike a real IFA she had not spent years gaining her spurs and sitting exams, she'd done a crash course to learn her commodity… money and how to launder it. That's what elite undercover officers do. Settling into the witness box behind a screen shielding her from the public and press, Sam turned to the judge, the Recorder of London and gave him an almost indiscernible nod of respect. Those in the know may have noticed a subtle nod from the judge. Then the bailiff approached and asked her if she wished to affirm or swear on the bible. Before she answered, Sam glanced across at the twelve men and women who made up the jury. She was ready, a little nervous as always, but confident she had performed her undercover role within the rules of evidence and the rule of law.

Was it almost two years ago? Sam's thoughts drifted off to an earlier time.

Raking through designer clothing in one of the many shops at Bicester Outlet Village, her phone rang. Sam was still thinking about earlier that day and her evidence at Oxford Crown Court over a job to do with a firm of armed robbers. She had rented a lock-up next to them to infiltrate, befriend, monitor, and inform on them. The robbers were good company to be around, but they were robbers, and she was an undercover cop. *Sorry boys, I guess I won't be getting a Christmas card this year, unlike last year,* Sam thought. It was JW, her cover officer, on the phone. *Do I let it go to answer phone or take it? My time at this precise moment is focused on clothing, not you, JW. Leave a message, I'll listen to it between shops.*

That's what she did. 'You have one new message, today at two twenty-one' her voicemail announced.

"Hi, Sam. If I was a betting man, right now I'll wager you are shopping in that designer outlet near Oxford. I got your message to say you have been released from court, thanks. Did their cover team look after you all right? When you get a minute give me a bell, nothing urgent, tomorrow will do when you are driving back home. Have a good night tonight with the op team. Cheers, stay safe mate."

'*To listen to the message again press...*' Sam didn't need to hear that automated voice anymore. She often thought it was like having two husbands with JW as her cover officer. He knew her almost as well as Ken used to, her ex. Sam believed he could even read her mood when she walked into the office and used this skill to his full advantage.

The drive home was okay. Sam only encountered a couple of blokes who thought their cars were an extension of their penises. *Tossers*, she thought. She called JW and arranged to meet in town at their favourite café after she had visited the gym and worked off the curry and bubbles from the night out with the op team. Sam always took her red gym bag with her; it was part of her deployment gear.

"What do you know about money laundering, Sam?" JW asked. "I know your old man used to be in the game, did you pick any bits and pieces up from him?"

Sam thought for a few seconds. "What? Ken's a washer of money? He's my ex, you should know better than calling him my old man."

"I'll rephrase," JW said. "Your ex, he's in finance, right?"

"I'm kidding, I know some of the language they use, words and phrases. I heard enough from Ken. What's this all about, what are we looking at, JW?" she asked raising her coffee cup to her lips and looking over the brim of the cup into his dark brown eyes.

JW put his cup down and took a deep breath. "I have been involved in a couple of meetings over the last few weeks with the boss about an international, multi-agency bit of work that they are trying to put together. One of the tactics they are looking at is an undercover deployment into the subjects. Nothing has been agreed yet. The commodity is money. Money laundering to be precise. It involves a core nominal who seems to pay tax on an income of twenty-three thousand pounds a year and lives in a small flat in South London. That's all bollocks. In short, he is washing his money from bent sales of properties, villas, apartments and complexes in Spain, Portugal, and the Canaries. The red flashing light for us, and I mean red light is the killing of the nominal's money man. He was shot dead outside a restaurant on the Costa del Sol. Professional hit, two guys on a motorbike, two shots in the head.

"The Spanish old bill, National Police Corps, the CNP, aren't knocking themselves out investigating. Just another dead dodgy Brit as far as they are concerned. MI6 have an input as do MI5, Customs, Serious Fraud Office, City of London Police, National Crime Squad, Uncle Tom Cobley and all. I don't think it's a runner to be honest, Sam, but if it is an option on the table, I want us to be ahead and waiting with a game plan up our sleeve, ready to go."

Sam had experienced numerous discussions over the years with bosses, other UCOs and cover officers about 'possible jobs' and they never materialised, and that's what she thought about this one. She has a phrase *'Too many moving parts'* and this had too many. "Well, sweetie, what is it you are saying to me? Why are you here right now talking about a job you don't think will happen?" Sam was trying not to sound disappointed at the suggestion that JW thought it was a nonrunner.

JW continued explaining his thoughts. "I Just wanted to put it on your radar, Sam, and ask you to have a think and perhaps take a bit of time researching the role and what you would need to know to carry it off. You certainly look the part; you could walk the walk and talk the talk. You could have a chat with your ex, pick his brains. You know what to do. Give it some thought, you've got some down time now, you might as well fill it with something. What do you say?"

And that was about two years ago. Because of Ken, Sam had some knowledge of IFAs, so that was a start. 'Know your commodity' was a piece of advice she was given as a UCO and that applied to everything; drugs, guns, fags, booze, and money.

So, with her inner dogged determination she set about learning how to be an IFA. Sam initially went to Ken. He knew her job and didn't ask the bleeding obvious. She also knew a couple of mates from the gym. Sue had her own company and was a fully qualified IFA and Stewart had worked in overseas investments and knew the system inside out. The problem with Sue and Stewart was they thought Sam worked for the Civil Service as a National Training Officer; hence the reason she was on the missing list from time to time. Sam hated telling lies to friends, but with what she did for a living, needs must sometimes. Sam came up with a cover story about a training course she was putting together about money laundering and needed to understand the subject better.

She invited them both to a coffee in the lounge bar at the gym after a workout so she could pick their brains. Stewart volunteered to speak on the course in relation to international legislation and Sue wanted to come along for the ride and a few drinks in the bar in the evenings. After a couple of weeks of researching Google, grilling Ken, and pumping Sue and Stewart for information, she was almost satisfied with her commodity knowledge if she ever needed to use it.

That's the thing: almost is not good enough. And she told JW as much. He came up trumps and put her in touch with Rosie Horgan, an assets recovery expert with the Regional Crime Squad. She was used to untangling a web of false money trails involving shell companies and offshore banking. Sam and Rosie became good friends. So much so, Rosie's tutorials took place at Sam's home with the bonus that Rosie turned out to be a first class cook specialising in Italian peasant dishes. And if push came to shove, Rosie didn't mind the odd bit of babysitting if Sam's mum or Ken weren't available.

So, back to today, the Old Bailey, number one court, and all the jurors' eyes fixed on Sam. What did they see and what did they think? They saw a mature woman, attractive, physically fit, blonde hair in a sophisticated 'up style', clear painted nails and light make-up, in a two-piece dark navy suit. They saw a professional businesswoman. Sam often thought about what went through their minds when they heard what she did, how she conducted herself when it got tense and dangerous. She could almost hear their minds ticking – *She looks like the woman who lives across the street.* She *was* that person who lives across the street for some of the time. But at other times, she was Detective Constable Samantha Smith, undercover police officer.

The defendants were sitting in the dock on the opposite side of the court room from her as Sam was about to give her evidence in chief. They were Andrew James Cooper, known to her as Andy or Coops, and Sergio Lopez, aka 'The Spaniard.'

Sam took the Bible and card from the bailiff. Holding the Bible high in her right hand, she glanced at the words on the card, but didn't need to read them. Sam recited the oath from memory in a strong, confident manner, just like on the many previous occasions. As the bailiff retrieved the Bible and card, she deliberately looked at Coops and the Spaniard. It was only for a second or two, but enough so she could see and sense the betrayal and hate in their eyes. Sam stared back to show her lack of fear or intimidation.

Coops could have avoided his day in court, well, three weeks in court as it turned out. He should have listened to Mr Terrence Walker, his private investigator, the PI. Sam could honestly say without fear of contradiction it was one of the most challenging and frightening times she had faced as a UCO. Not just the car chase but having to confront Coops knowing what they both knew. During that meeting, they were in a high-stake poker game. Both were cheating but Sam had to keep her game face on and try to bluff her way through.

Chapter 2

What Makes Them Tick?

Assistant Chief Constable Mark Edwards was addressing a steering committee of the College of Policing at a secluded country hotel in the heart of England. He had special responsibility for Authorised Professional Practice in the field of undercover or covert policing. In readiness for the dissolution of ACPO, the Association of Chief Police Officers, and the new replacement body, the National Police Chiefs' Council, NPCC, Edwards knew a review of the selection and monitoring of undercover officers would remain high on the agenda of any future government Home Office minister given the continuing adverse publicity surrounding the ongoing public inquiry into undercover policing in England and Wales.

He had spent the previous year liaising with overseas law enforcement agencies including the FBI, Canada's RCMP, and the Dutch police delving into their operating procedures for undercover policing including what they had learnt about the selection and training of these officers deployed on covert policing. Those gathered knew Edwards was an expert in this field. They listened closely to what he had to say.

"The selection of officers suitable for this type of work is of vital importance. So are the structures to monitor performances throughout their undercover careers. That is to say, monitoring of not only their effectiveness in the field but also their fitness, their mental health... psychological wellness... if you like. These are key in this type of work which can be dangerous and stressful by its very nature.

"Fortunately, I found two experienced undercover officers who were willing to cooperate in discussing their careers with Paul Nuemann, the distinguished psychologist, who many of you will know. At the beginning of the sessions, they were close to retirement and indeed continued the sessions even after their retirement dates. The results were enlightening, and my recommendation is their profiles are used as benchmarks in future selection and training for the next generation of UCOs, with this caveat: they are both white British, IC1s. It may be the case for ethnic minorities these benchmarks will need some tweaking and adjustments.

"You will hear in a narrative fashion and in their own words, the formative years and backgrounds of these two officers. Usually, in this type of situation, we would be using only their national index numbers but I feel strongly that would depersonalise the exercise so they will be referred to by their operational cover names of Dominic, Dom, and Samantha, Sam, Smith. Yes, same family name because they ended up as partners under the same roof as well as partners on some undercover deployments. Once you have heard from them, you will understand just what made them tick. Just why they appeared serene on the outside whilst using coping mechanisms to combat the stresses of their roles and internal turmoil. I'll now hand over to Paul."

"Good morning, for those who don't know me my name is Paul Nuemann. I am a clinical and forensic psychologist with a special interest in undercover policing with numerous peer-reviewed publications to my name in that field. You will hear me read the narrative accounts of Dominic and Samantha Smith. I'm sorry to say there are no copies available for you for reasons of security. The narratives were compiled by me following numerous one-on-one interviews with each officer separately and done with their full consent. They are quite lengthy so we are scheduled to meet here again tomorrow morning to complete the exercise but you are aware of that."

Chapter 3

Samantha Session One

MANY YEARS AFTER THE Jack Tar bust and both before and after Dom and I had retired, we were asked to cooperate with a College of Policing project. We agreed because we were told it would help the future generation of undercover officers. This is what we said throughout many meetings with the project coordinator.

I love my job. I hate the journey. But who would have bet on me working behind enemy lines as an undercover police officer (UCO) and ending up as the CEO of my own security company, certainly not me or anyone I grew up around?

I travel along the same roads between my home and the office maybe two or three times a week depending on my timetable and meetings. I set off early morning to beat the traffic build-up and enjoy the quiet time to reflect on events past and present.

"Tosser," I shout out as a bloke driving a van pulls out from lane one into lane two cutting me up on the dual carriageway. I think *He's getting the one finger bird when I speed past him at my first opportunity.* I don't know if the van man or the 'tosser' driving up my exhaust pipe or trying to undertake me further along the road would be at the top of my list of drivers I would gladly castrate. I know how they think. They see a middle-aged, attractive blonde driving a nice motor as an easy touch to dominate and hassle - me Tarzan, you Jane, get out of my way. Not this girl mister.

Dom, my partner in life for too many years to remember describes me as a 'flash bang' one of those hand grenades Special Forces use when they are storming a building. They go off without warning and cause mayhem. He says, "At least with a conventional grenade it has a fuse before it explodes, you just go off without warning." Oh, and he describes my cooking style as flambé as the smoke alarm, which I use as a timer, constantly goes off when I'm in the kitchen. He knows when he's telling that 'made up' story it winds me up, but he still tells it. He's a great storyteller and uses his natural sense of humour when explaining what it is like living with me.

We are both alphas and have strong personalities. We needed them in our line of work. Our relationship is best described as fiery which keeps it fresh. We can argue about anything at the drop of a hat. I hate being told what to do and how to do it. This is probably a hangover from being a mum bringing up a child while holding down a demanding job in a male-dominated environment. I must add that I was a single mum for a long time after my divorce from Ken.

On route to my office, I pass the slip road I use to take when dropping my son James off at school. That was a few years ago now. I will always be indebted to my mum and dad for stepping in for me with childcare support and the school run when I was away on a job (an undercover operation). Even after the divorce, Ken, James's dad moved close by and did his share of looking after James in periods of my absence. It was a bit like a juggling act at times especially when I got called upon at short notice, but we managed. The last thing I wanted to say to my bosses was that I was not available because I was a single mum with childcare issues. I had fought many hard battles to get where I was, and I was not going to give those that doubted me the pleasure of saying, "I told you so." No chance. I look across the sports field towards his old school and for some reason, my mind slips back to attending sports day. It was the first time Dom met James. It was a warm summer's day with a slight breeze blowing across the sports field of James's public school.

Lots of yummy mummies as I call them or ladies that do lunch, were stood around dressed in their specially purchased outfits, talking about their recent visit to the gym or shopping expedition. Dads in groups of equal sizes blowing smoke up their own backsides exchanging belly laughs and stories about their last trip or business conquest. Today I'm just a plain and simple mum to James in year six. Nothing unusual in the role or title of mum for a female. Males or dads, females or mums, are equals, well sometimes. It depends on what world you are living in at the time. Like all the other mums I am there cheering my son on in his efforts to be awarded a 'congratulations for taking part in the race' certificate. It may rub some people up the wrong way but, in my book, it's winning that matters, not the taking part. Those that come second are the first losers in my rule book of life. This rule of life I have instilled into James since the day he was born. The mums' and dads' races are planned to take place towards the end of the afternoon.

Dom challenged me to enter. "You're having a laugh, in these shoes and a skirt?" I said, giving him what he calls 'the eyes.' It is a look I have and give out to people that say 'tosser' without the use of words.

Not one to duck a challenge and being extremely fit, plus the fact I have my gym kit in the boot of the car I say, "Let's do it." I disappear and return a few minutes later in trainers and trackie bottoms. Not doing much for my appearance but I'm not entering a fashion show, I am here to win. I remember before the race started when all the mums are gathering at the start line egging each other on. Because of the nature of my job, I always kept myself to myself and avoided getting involved in the banter. I would give a polite 'hello' to the odd familiar face at drop off or pick up time, but I didn't engage.

Can you imagine how the conversation would go? 'Hi, Sam, what is it you do for a living?'

I reply, 'I'm an undercover police officer.' I can hear their clipped well-to-do voices and see their faces immaculately made-up with lippy, eye liner and foundation.

'Gosh, that must be super exciting, tell me do you carry a gun?'

I think back to my early days as a UCO someone once said to me, 'The easiest question to answer is the one that's never asked.' The advice continued, 'so don't allow the bad guys or girls to ask it.'

The games teacher, Mr Brownlow, a fit-looking fella in his late twenties with a healthy tan, sporting white tennis shorts and a colour-matched polo shirt, looking every bit the part of eye candy to a few of the younger yummy mummies, calls the 'ladies' to the start line. I look up and down the line trying to work out who the first loser is going to be. I already know who is going to win.

"On your marks. Get set. Go!" shouted the teacher.

I got off to a flying start totally focused on the winning line eighty metres in front of me. I powered my five foot nine, fit, slim toned body down the track. In my peripheral vision, I could see my challenger. We were neck and neck thundering down the track like two Olympic sprinters. *God knows where the rest are, are we the only two to have started?* No time to waste on thoughts, focus and drive on. With the last ten metres closing, I kicked like Florence Griffith-Joyner in the 1998 Olympic games and smashed the school record. Sam, mother of James year six and an enigma to everyone is the fastest mum on two legs. In the interest of maintaining good relationships, I politely accept my certificate congratulating me on' taking part.' *Bloody hell, I did not take part, I won*, I thought as Mr Brownlow shook my hand and presented the certificate.

James is now in his twenties. He's smart, polite, handsome, I would say that, wouldn't I? He's also well grounded. He has had a good education with support from his dad and oozes confidence. When in the safe company of family and close friends that knew what type of cop I was, James tells the stories of being a child in the life of an undercover mum. If anyone asked what his mum did for a living, he was instructed to tell them his mum files papers in an office.

Being driven round roundabouts two or three times before exiting was a natural occurrence in his younger years. If I noticed a car in my rear-view mirror that had been in convoy with us for a couple of turns, I would go into anti and counter-surveillance mode. When he was old enough to reason things out for himself, he wouldn't even raise his head or ask what I was doing. His command of the English language, particularly some old Anglo-Saxon words and 'tosser' were beyond his years. He took full advantage of this by introducing a swear box that lived in the car glovebox. At the end of a journey, he would take the box out and billed me for my language.

One of his favourite stories is when I was stopped by a traffic cop for an alleged minor moving traffic offence. James was sat in the front passenger seat. As the traffic officer approached the car, I rolled the window down. The officer stated the reason for the stop, and I got into complete denial.

During the exchange of words, the officer said, "Look don't piss me about."

That was my get out of jail free card. I got out of the car and said words to the effect of 'How dare you to use language like that in front of my son?' The officer backed down, apologised, and left me to go on my way.

As I got back into the car James opened the glovebox and said, "Just as well he didn't look in here, Mum." The box was emptied regularly and the contents were put into his savings account. Dom reckons he probably could have bought his own house by the age of ten.

Being a child growing up with no dad in the house give me the added responsibility of performing both roles, mum and dad.

His dad is a good man. It just did not work out for us. He has always been in James's life and supported him in every possible way. Why did it not work out? If I was to put my hand on my heart, I would blame my focus on my career. Being married to a female police officer, particularly a driven and ambitious one that does not take no for an answer, could not have been easy for him. He had his own successful insurance business which could not have been more different to that of a police officer. The divorce rate amongst cops must be in the top ten of occupations that suffer the pain of a marriage breakdown. I had an added ingredient in my cake. Not only was I a cop, but I also worked as an undercover police officer, sometimes playing the role of a girlfriend or wife of some other guy. Sharing a flat, house or hotel room with some other guy. Going to fine dining restaurants having meals with some other guy and going onto the best clubs in town rubbing shoulders with celebrities and the bad guys and girls. I was constantly mixing with crooks, organised crime groups, OCGs, the top echelon of crooks in the UK and Europe and usually with some other guy who happened to be another undercover officer. My mantra was to beat the villains at their own game and on their own turf. I received certificates in the form of Chief Constables Commendations for winning, not for just taking part, for putting bad men and women behind bars for years. Ask yourself, how would your old man respond to you telling him you were off to Spain with another guy for a few weeks? How do you think that would land let alone the danger of the role? On some operations, I would deploy solo. These roles are tricky as the bad guys could cry foul at trial and claim a honey trap such as the case surrounding Colin Stagg and the female UCO Lizzie. So, these types of deployments must be managed with the utmost care by the cover officer and operational team.

I had enough to think about when working: rules of evidence, agent provocateur, direct questions, how much I am drinking? Is the recording device working? What did the target just say? Did I hear him right? Fuck, I've got bloody parents' evening tomorrow, mum's at the hospital for her check-up, Dom wants us to go to a BBQ at the weekend with friends and guess what, it's that time of the month.

Being a single mum in a male-dominated environment within the job and even more so on the plot with people that do not have political correctness or the same values as you comes with its own challenges. I love a challenge and a verbal scrap. I loved tucking my boy up at night and calling him 'Bedbug' as I kissed him on his tiny smooth forehead. I loved being an undercover cop and everything that came with it. I loved both worlds and found a way of meshing them together without causing harm or damage to James but chasing and catching a dream.

As Dom says, "Only one person is stopping you from doing what you want to do, and that is you."

With those words in mind, I believe that mantra has been part of my success since an early age.

Chapter 4

Samantha Session Two

"THERE WILL BE AIR miles in this job," Dom said to me and Phil when we signed up for Operation Candle. This was an operation that Dom had taken from the first conception to a fully mature adult, guiding and advising senior officers and an operational team in the technique of infiltrating busy criminal communities using Phil and me as the principal UCOs. It was his baby and had matured to deliver results. Two and a half years after he had mentioned Airmiles, I, together with Dom and Phil, was sitting in a Gatwick airport lounge waiting for our flight to Miami via New York's JFK. Dom and Phil raised their glasses of red wine. I raised my glass of bubbles. "Cheers, team. Told you there would be air miles in this job," Dom said with that 'told you so' smirk on his face.

Looking out beyond Dom through the large window, I could see an aircraft manoeuvring onto a stand. Deep in thought, I found myself asking a question - *How did you get here girl?*

I recalled the girl who was denied the opportunity to sit 'O'-levels at school because of my behaviour and total lack of commitment and effort. Then fast-forwarded to where I am now, the CEO of my own security company. I have had to fight, overcome challenges, and prove myself to others every step of the way. My determination and tenacity had been developed from a very young age.

I'm the eldest of three, I have a younger brother, Noel and a sister, Nina. As the eldest, I was left in charge when mum went off to work at the local school as a dinner lady with her second job as a cleaner in an office block. Dad worked as a handyman in a large factory. We never had much as kids, but we never wanted for anything, unlike Dom's humble and difficult early years. After school and during school holidays, in the absence of mum and dad, I was the boss, organiser and protector of my siblings as well as the cook for the family's evening meal. We called it 'tea' back in the day, 'dinner' now I'm a captain of industry. These devolved responsibilities became the foundations and building blocks for my attitude in life. It prepared me for battles I would have to fight in my personal life and my career as a cop. I thrived on the faith, trust, and confidence my parents had in me as I did in later life from SIOs as an undercover officer.

In my teenage years, I was drawn towards punk fashion, music, and hair colouring, which did not sit well with my parents or schoolteachers. I did not care that I was disturbing the environment or drawing unwarranted attention to myself. It didn't matter to me then, in fact, I liked it. This was totally opposite to my thought processes as an undercover officer. It's what I wanted, and no one was going to tell me I couldn't do it or stop me from doing it. During my punk period, I became a rebel and fell out with those that did not see my side of the argument. My parents and school were the main victims of this attitude. I was now a teenager and didn't need parents or teachers anymore. I was independent and capable of looking after myself. I loved being outdoors, camping out in nearby fields and riding horses bareback. Well, if you don't own the horse then how do you get a saddle and a bridle? I suppose I was what some people might call a bit wild. I decided I was going to move out of the family home as soon as possible. I don't know where it came from or if anyone put the idea in my head, but I had heard that police cadets did things like climb tors, took part in canoe races, camping and all the things I enjoyed. Plus, they even got paid for doing it and were provided with free accommodation. It was what I call a 'no brainer' so I contacted my local police force and enquired about becoming a police cadet.

My newly developed independence ran into a massive problem. The police recruitment sergeant told me I needed four 'O'-levels. I had already messed up my reputation and support from the school. I had told my parents I was moving out and didn't need their parental care. Now, I found I needed both education and my parents' support. This was my first lesson in not burning bridges. My teacher had already decided that I was only worthy of sitting for CSEs because of my truanting, attitude and lack of commitment and effort. I needed four 'O'-levels and my parents' support, or my escape plan was out the window. I cleaned up my appearance, changed my purple hair to an acceptable shade of blonde and practised in front of my bedroom mirror looking regretful, committed, and practising my lines in preparation for the meeting between me, my parents and Mr Howard, the headteacher. On the day of the meeting, I had my role and appearance off to a tee. Together with my parents, I had to get Mr Howard to change his mind and go against the advice of his teaching staff and allow me to join the sixth form. Not dissimilar to my undercover role in the Jack Tar drugs buy which I was to do many years later. The plan worked and I entered the sixth form and focused for the next year on not four but five 'O' levels and passed with A and B grades. I also got two passes at 'A' level. Thanks, mum and dad for your support. I probably did not deserve it and a big thank you to Mr Howard for having trusted me. Had he stuck to his previous decision, I often wonder where life would have taken me.

With my five 'O' and two 'A' levels, I joined the police cadets aged eighteen. I loved all the outside activities, thriving on these and took a leading role in team events and support activities within the community. I didn't enjoy or participate in the initiation ceremonies. It would come under the heading of bullying in today's parlance. I recall one of these childish ceremonies which involved the senior male cadets who had joined the previous year. They coerced the ten female cadets in my junior intake to do a fashion type parade in their underwear around the common room of the cadets' accommodation block. I was the only girl to tell them to "fuck off" and stood my ground alone, not for the last time in my career, against arrogant, ego-driven male chauvinists.

After one year I was sworn in as a real cop and was posted to work in a busy city. I did the normal general patrol tasks and did not dodge the punch ups and nicking arseholes and quickly found I had a reputation with my managers as a no-messing strong thief-taking character who could talk to the bad guys and girls on their level. As a result, I became well known for getting 'coughs', admissions in formal obtaining informants and I was delighted to find out from a core nominal that he and members of an OCG referred to me as the 'Wolf in sheep's clothing'. I was approached by a DS from the Specialist Operations Department who thought I would be a good candidate for a Test Purchase role (TP). These were cops that worked undercover buying drugs in small personal quantities on the streets from low-level drug dealers. After completing a few interviews and passing the TP course I did several 'buys' mainly of charlie (cocaine). I developed the persona of a classy professional female that enjoyed some of Colombia's finest marching powder. The body counts on these operations were always in double figures and consisted of doormen, posh blokes at nightclubs and dealers in pubs who had the knowledge and blessing of the landlord. Many a landlord lost his job and accommodation for a kickback from a dealer.

I met Ken, my ex, at a friend's garden party. He wasn't a cop which didn't seem to matter at first. We hit it off straight away and found ourselves very quickly in an intense relationship. Before we knew it, we were planning our wedding and bought our first house together. I was focused on my career and not on my marriage and relationship with Ken. At work, I had been recruited onto the newly formed Major Crime Unit, investigating high profile murders, kidnaps, conducting surveillance and carrying out Test Purchase deployments for other Police forces as well as my own force. Even though I was 'full on' in terms of my work commitments I still found time for the gym, swimming, dancing and socialising with my colleagues. I never took my eye off the ball in my work life and my relationship with Ken paid the price. I was so active and fit I didn't even know I was four months pregnant. Five months later James entered my world. After our divorce, Ken and I remained good friends and he supported and continues to support his son in every way.

After maternity leave, I returned to the job. Instantly I detected a sea change in attitudes towards me. I had too much baggage, a mum with a new born baby. I felt I had to prove myself all over again within a male-dominated job. I was no longer getting the prolonged enquiries or the opportunity to work overtime or away overnight. Instead, I was handed the mundane house to house or collection of CCTV duties. I had not sat idle during my maternity leave. I'd organised a nursery place for James, childcare arrangements with my parents and Ken, and a part-time nanny to support me. My world was no different to a male colleague who had a new born and a wife at home. *Bollocks, I'm not having this, time to challenge people's attitude towards me*, I thought. I started with my DS and DI who both collapsed like a paper house in a rainstorm when I confronted them. I didn't have to take it any further. Both men knew me well and realised I would take my grievance all the way to the top if I had to. Had I wanted 'special treatment,' I would have asked for it. I never asked and I didn't want it. Normal service was resumed instantly.

The next three years were challenging on occasions juggling a home, a child, a demanding job and all the other stuff that comes with being a parent. I was still doing TP work and had one eye on doing the full-blown level one undercover course. I wanted a new challenge for myself. I found out using my own initiative where to obtain an application form from. Back in those days, most undercover officers were recruited from specialist squads not from a force Major Crime Unit. But I'm Sam, and if Sam wants it enough, Sam will get it. Once in possession of the application, I completed it citing all my skills, knowledge and qualifications and listed the certificates of merit and Chief Constable commendations. I booked an appointment with my DI as he would have to support my application. I had no reason to think he would not support my application, after all, I had been doing a first-class job for him and worked on several high-profile cases. This proved to be his reason for not supporting me. His words are imprinted in my memory, "You're one of the best detectives I've got on this unit, Sam, and I've no doubt you'll get through all the hoops and complete the course with flying colours. But I don't want to lose you. The role is far more demanding than TP work and you're a mum with a young child. It's not for you, Sam, I'm sorry but I'm not supporting your application."

The fact that he referred to me being a mum really got under my skin. Before leaving his office, I asked him one more time if he would reconsider. I wasn't going to plead with him I had my plan 'B' all ready to go. He refused to change his mind. "Hope you don't mind, boss, but I'm going to push this as far as I can, thanks for your time," I said.

Through my well-known work ethics, conscientiousness and achievements within the Major Crime Unit and TP work, I had come to the notice of the SLT, the Senior Leadership Team, of the force and I had a great working relationship with the Assistant Chief Constable (Crime), head of CID. I came out of the DI's office and found an empty office with a phone. I called the head of CID's secretary and asked for an appointment with the ACC at a convenient time for him. I was asked what the nature of the appointment was and just left it as a personal matter. It's almost unheard of for a DC to request a meeting with an ACC but this was Detective Constable Samantha Smith, and she had the balls to ask and 'if you don't ask you don't get'.

My appointment was arranged for the following day in a conference room at HQ. I made some excuse to leave the office and made my way to HQ. On entering the conference room, the boss and his secretary were sitting side by side at the large conference table with sheets of A4 paper scattered on it. The boss stood up and reached out his right hand. We shook hands and greeted each other with a friendly smile. He asked if it was okay for his secretary to stay, or would I prefer she left. I informed him I had no issue with her staying. I've always been confident and able to engage with any officer regardless of their seniority. I detailed my conversation with my DI the previous day tactfully and diplomatically and said I felt I was being held back for all the wrong reasons. Firstly, for being too good at my job and secondly because I was a mother. Professionally I knew I was in a strong position and the DI's reasoning wouldn't hold water. The ACC asked all the right questions about my strategy for dealing with the demands of the selection process and the role. I was able to satisfy him on all counts. The meeting lasted almost half an hour, twenty-five minutes longer than the meeting with the DI. He told me to complete the application and he would speak with my boss. I was a little uncomfortable bypassing the DI, but I was determined to test myself at the highest level of policing.

My selection process followed the same path as that of Dom. After jumping through the many hoops, I found myself on the NUTAC. I was the only female on my course but that didn't faze me one bit. I'd often been the lone female in a male-dominated profession. At the outset of the course, I was assigned a course tutor. The role of the tutor was to offer guidance and you could seek advice during the course. A guy by the name of Roland, who liked to be called Rolo, was assigned to me. This guy, who clearly thought he was 'God's gift to women' from his head-to-toe designer clothing, which was ten years too young for him, through to the misogynistic conversations I overheard him having with other instructors. He didn't even speak to me all the way through the course until the last night when we were having a celebratory drink in some wine bar. Rolo came up to me, "I guess you are wondering why I haven't spoken to you during the course, Sam."

I looked at him with contempt, and replied with one word, "No." then I turned and walked away. He must have hated that! Rolo and I were to cross paths on a few occasions in the following years, but we never exchanged numbers or sent each other a Christmas card.

On successfully completing the course, I returned to my day job waiting for the phone to ring with my first bit of work. Meanwhile, I began to build a legend and obtain all the documentation I would need to survive as a level one UCO.

Chapter 5

Dominic Session One

I WAS FAMILIAR WITH the sound of the slow drag of the train's engine as it gained speed pulling out of London Euston train station and disappeared into the pitch-black tunnel for a few seconds, passing under some part of north London taking me back to my childhood stomping grounds in the north of England. Dominic Smith or Dom as I am known to my friends, on the face of it appeared no different to the reflection I was staring at in the train window.

Why should it?

The reflection staring back at me was the same age as me, the early sixties wearing fashionable designer glasses. He had a healthy tanned complexion, together with silver hair that gave the impression he used designer salons to keep it looking good. He had the appearance and bearing of a prosperous man, which was no illusion.

I had been very successful in both my career as a military man and as a police officer. I was physically fit, had a bit of a gut which I had developed over the years with the assistance of good food, wine, beer, and a love of Irish whiskey. I was in good health, no problems with mobility, unlike many of my former military mates and retired cops whose hips or knees or both had been replaced. One guy who was four years younger than me had three of the four joints replaced and was waiting for the second knee op to complete the set. I do not display any outward signs that would suggest I was on a hospital waiting list anytime soon. The small red and white pills that sit, for most of the time, on my tidy bedside table, unlike Samantha's, Sam as I call her, my life partner. Her bedside table is best described as a bric-a-brac tabletop at a jumble sale. I take the pill every night like clockwork for high blood pressure. I have taken my 'Samantha Pill' for more years than I can remember. I jokingly renamed the Ramipril pill the Samantha pill as she is, in my humble opinion, the main reason for any symptoms that lead to high blood pressure in my comfortable life.

My preferred dress style is smart casual: chinos, brown leather belts, brogue shoes, my favourite shoes are brown. I always took my time to ensure my choice of socks didn't clash with the shoes and chinos. Nothing more eye-catching than a bloke wearing the wrong-coloured socks with his ensemble. In my mind, it would disturb the environment and attract unwanted attention. 'Not disturbing the environment' was once an integral part of my life. My choice of shirt is either a polo shirt or an open neck dress shirt with a button-down collar in a pastel colour. Pinks and blues are high on my list of favourite colours. I have a collection of designer Italian Cavani jackets. This design has contrasting, eye-catching stitching around the lapels and pockets and always draws complementary comments from the company when out and about with Sam.

As the train reaches its cruising speed passing under tunnels and through deep railway cuttings my reflection in the window disappears without warning and reappears in a blink of the eye. It is a reminder of my fifteen years as an undercover police officer, UCO. Here one minute, gone the next. For some periods during the train journey, as in my undercover life, I could see my reflection for prolonged periods. Much the same as the criminals and organised crime groups I had infiltrated would have seen me. I was exposed to them, in open sight, with no protection of a uniform, or colleagues at the other end of a radio. I had no baton, handcuffs, incapacitant spray or taser. I certainly had no gun. I was armed only with my specialist undercover training, an innate ability to think on my feet at speed and my years of police experience. These, together with my young life, upbringing, my military career, and allied to the fact that I could talk my way into or out of situations stood me in good stead. I also had the priceless ability to fit into different settings and scenarios without disturbing the criminal and violent environments I sometimes inhabited. A chameleon, I guess.

Some of the time, owing to the direction of travel or the sunlight, there wasn't a reflection to be seen. The other guy, whatever his name was, had gone. Where did he go? What was he doing when he was not there? These are the sort of questions many criminals asked me or themselves whether out of curiosity, interest, or suspicion. I always had an answer ready - keep the lie as close to the truth as possible. I was told that back in the early days of my undercover life because it was easier to remember that way. I was a dad and a husband. I had family commitments and responsibilities the same as every other man. I had childcare issues, Christmas plays, parents' evenings, family holidays and celebrations. I was not only expected to attend and support my family, but it was also my duty to do so. When the reflection was not there, I was enjoying a home and family life. I took my son to football, drove my daughter and her friends to town and collected them when asked. I did 'dad stuff'. When out with my wife, dinner with friends, BBQ in the back garden, on holidays and the dreaded DIY, I was doing the 'husband stuff'. I enjoyed going to the pub with my mates, watched football, played golf. I did normal stuff with normal people. It was me that was different. I was an undercover police officer.

Of the fifteen years I worked in covert operations I wouldn't be undercover every day. As already explained, I had commitments outside my police role, but I would always have to be contactable by my Senior Investigating Officer, SIO, and the bad guys at any time. I could not just disappear from the operational area, known as the plot in the trade, for periods and just reappear by dropping in 'out of the sky'. I also always had several mobile phones around me. I often found myself deployed on several undercover jobs at the same time. Some of the undercover roles I performed were minor 'walk on, walk off' parts. In other operations, I took on the role of the principal UCO. I gained extensive experience and knowledge in undercover tactics and respect from all in undercover policing over the years and took on additional roles as a cover officer and tactical advisor to SIOs when required.

Despite my thoughts on the train, I kept my antenna up and remained aware of who was around me and what was occurring. I had reserved the best seat in the carriage to control the comings and goings of other passengers. Not that I was worried about any threat to me; it was a habit, it's called trade craft. I had developed this skill as a police officer when carrying out surveillance but especially working undercover. As a UCO I ensured I was ahead and waiting for the operational target to arrive at a meeting or as he/she was entering a venue such as a bar or a restaurant. What's the saying? Old habits die hard. Sam and I are often noticed quickening our pace and looking for the shortest route to our restaurant table. Our style of covering the ground is reminiscent of that strange walking style adopted by speed walkers at an athletics meeting. Not quite a run but not far off. We are both focused on occupying the seat that gives us the best control of the room and never sitting with our back to the other diners. It's every man or woman for themselves on these occasions, no quarter is given, and none is expected between us.

I settled down into the journey which with today's modern trains takes around two hours to cover just over two hundred miles. Far quicker than my early memories when I travelled the same route with a leave pass in my pocket. That was a very different Dom. Back in the day, I would be in the company of other lads heading home. We would grab something to eat and drink from the shops on the station concourse. A diet of sandwiches, cold pork pies, chocolate bars, crisps, and a few cans of lager or beer to wash it down with. Being servicemen, we knew how to conduct ourselves. We could chat and exchange banter with each other whilst respecting our fellow travellers. We would not attract attention or adverse comments by loutish behaviour or using loud bad language. We were disciplined, members of Her Majesty's Armed Forces and conducted ourselves accordingly, in or out of uniform. I am still in touch with some of those guys, others have regrettably passed, some were killed while serving, others have unfortunately slipped into the fog of my memory banks. That was over forty years ago, they and I have moved on and hopefully made something out of our lives.

The discipline instilled into me as a soldier was another means in the toolbox of life that I would use and depend on in my police and undercover career. I smile as I recall some of the journeys and squaddie (soldier) banter shared with my mates over the years. A sense of humour was another tool I have in my imaginary toolbox. I have a sharp wit and sense of humour. I use it to great effect without causing offence. I am quick thinking. I can come up with a line at the drop of a hat. There are no pregnant pauses or disjointed conversations with me. The conversations flowed in a very natural way in my undercover career. I engaged with many villains on a range of subjects from kilos of drugs to killing people, guns and bullets. And lorry loads of alcohol or cigarettes. When you engage in conversation with these criminals you cannot hesitate and stumble over your words and thoughts. You must be confident and natural, unfazed by their conversation about their future intentions and what they want. You must know your commodity or the service they are looking for and you are going to provide them with. It could be transport, storage, or financial facilities.

My train is just passing through Stockport and I'm coming to the end of my journey. Faster trains are not the only change, the skyline of Manchester has also changed. It is a cleaner modern city, and the skyline is populated with modern glass and steel structures. The Manchester Hilton Hotel is now one of the famous landmarks of the city and can be seen from miles away. This is my city and I love it, but I could not go back to living there for several reasons that I will address later. As well as my city it is home to my football team, Manchester United.

Chapter 6

Dominic Session Two

I AM ONE OF five children in my family who were dragged up in Manchester. When I try to explain my upbringing and family environment as a child to my loved ones, friends and my children, I draw the comparison to the TV programmes *Shameless* and the Chatsworth estate. I lived on a council estate in east Manchester which was very much like the Chatsworth estate. It was a tough part of town and seemed to house many people and families that could be described as dysfunctional. I include my family and my environment in that description.

I shared a bed with my brother and my clothes were hand me downs from my cousin who was a good six inches taller than me, and he had big feet. He sent me down a pair of winklepickers once, but I had to pack the toe with newspaper to keep them on my feet. The shoes had steel tips on the heel and toe which me sound like a lame horse as I walked along the street or up the stone staircases at school. After a week or so the toes packed with newspaper began to curl up, like Aladdin's shoes much to everyone's amusement. This was all character-building stuff. The police were regular visitors to my estate, going through someone's front door at six in the morning to effect an arrest or chasing someone who had been disturbed committing a burglary in a better part of town. Regardless of my relationship with the police in those days, somewhere in my DNA lay a latent desire to become a police officer, although I did not know it at the time.

As a child, we lived from hand to mouth, but my parents always seemed to have money for bingo in my mother's case and the pub, cards, and fruit machines in my father's. Everything in our house ran off a meter: the gas, electricity and the television. The meter took either a shilling coin, five pence in today's currency or a two-shilling coin, ten pence today. The cash meter was the forerunner to the card meters of today, where a customer hands a card and money to the shop assistant in the local shop and prepays for their gas or electricity. This method means the money used to purchase the power stays in the shop. In my day the meter had a securely fitted money box that was supposedly tampered proof. No, it was not. My parents found many ways to cheat and obtain free gas and electricity. The favourite was filing down an old half-penny to fit in the slot. The gas and electric companies overpriced the rates to meter users, and you would receive a rebate when the man came to empty it. The meter man would always give the half-pennies back in the rebate to be used another day. On the regular occasions when both my parents were out and the electricity went off because the meter had run out, we would knock at a neighbour's house and ask to borrow a shilling until my parents got home.

One of my memories and a story I often tell my friends and family over a few drinks or dinner is taking myself off for medical treatments at the age of nine or ten years of age. I would attend Accident and Emergency alone. No parent or responsible adult accompanying me or booking me in at reception. I did it myself. On one visit I had broken a bone in my foot, and they wanted to cut my shoe so it would fit around the splint. No way are you cutting my shoe. I managed to get back home on the bus and hopped with my shoe intact.

On another occasion when I was still at junior school, I had excruciating pain in my lower abdomen. My mum sent me off to the doctor's surgery alone. This was in the days when you did not need an appointment to see the doctor, you just turned up and took your turn in the queue. I was not even tall enough to see over the hatch that the receptionist sat behind. Looking up and into the hatch but only seeing the reception ceiling, I booked myself in and sat in the waiting room making a mental note of my position in the queue. On this occasion, the doctor gave me an internal examination of my rectum and diagnosed me as having appendicitis. Imagine your eight- or nine-year-old child or grandchild taking themself off to the doctor alone. Unimaginable today. I guess Social Services would be all over my parents today.

Both of my parents had jobs, but I recall from their many and constant verbal arguments and physical fights the phrase, 'It's my money and I'll spend it on what I want' referring to their wages. I have no recollection of the term domestic violence, which is widely used today, having ever entered the lexicon of my home. My parents had real fights, punching, kicking, hair pulling and an onslaught of verbal abuse. I would jump on my father's back to pull him off my mother but got cast aside like a ragdoll. Over the years, up until I was sixteen, I took a few beatings, from my father as a child, some deserved no doubt. I knew the impact of his open or closed hand and his size eight boots. The worst was bending over the seat of a chair and being lashed across my bare buttocks with a dog's lead. I was so terrified of this punishment and pain I would literally pee myself before he started and as he was administering the lashes. On my first leave and my return home from the Army, my father was play fighting with me. I had been trained in unarmed combat and dropped him on the rug like he was a piece of limp lettuce. He fell onto the carpet, cracking his elbow and damaging the chrome on the gas fire. That was the last time my father and I exchanged blows. I have never hit my children and they have all grown up to be successful and awesome individuals.

The kids I knocked about with were in the same boat as me. Everyone's family back then seemed to have lots of children.

I knew of families of seven, eight, nine and even ten children. This was the late sixties, early seventies and we all played in the street. You let the dog out the front door to roam the streets and poop wherever they wanted to. No one going behind the dog with a poop bag. There were no cars to worry about on the estate. I ran with a gang of lads that got up to the usual minor and more serious crime. I was not an angel by any means but growing up this way was an education I used in my undercover career. I became street smart. I had my brushes with the law on occasions but was able to talk my way out of any serious court appearances or jail time unlike some of my mates.

Even within our estate, there were certain streets you did not walk along alone. If you lived on Kings Road you would never walk along Queens Road, if you were spotted by a kid from an opposing gang, you would be attacked and take a few punches and kicks if you did not have the speed to getaway. For many years I was forced to walk along Queens Road because I had upset an ex-girlfriend and she told her older brother, Jimmy, who was five years older than me. Every time I walked down the street past their house, he would come out give me a load of verbal abuse, pick me up and throw me through the hedgerow of someone's front garden. It was a case of Hobson's choice, run like hell along Queens or hope Jimmy did not notice me.

From a very early age, I found myself a job firstly helping the local milkman and then a paper round. The couple that ran the paper shop really looked after me. I had a marvellous relationship with them. I did a paper round in the morning and night Monday to Saturday and on Sunday mornings. If one of the other lads did not turn in, they would give me the spare round, more money. I would work in the shop when I was not at school. No papers on Sunday evening, however, on Sunday afternoon I would caddy for George, the owner of the shop, at the golf club in an upmarket part of the city, miles away from where I lived. After the round, he would pay me and buy me Sunday dinner in the clubhouse. George and his lovely wife,

Doris looked after me and treated me extremely well. There are many components in me as a person and the life choices I have made, and they can be traced back to my relationship with those two wonderful people. They gave me a strong work ethic and showed me how working hard brings rewards. God bless them and I thank them.

Once, working for George and Doris, I turned up at six in the morning to mark up the papers, putting the different papers into piles with the door number on the top corner, for the various rounds before leaving to do my own round when I fell ill with a strong cramp type feeling in my lower abdomen. I also felt nauseous. George and Doris sent me home. My mother was in bed after a night shift at the hospital as an auxiliary nurse. I got on the sofa and curled up in pain and felt sick. My mother got up around eleven and sent me to school for my dinner and told me if I felt ill, I was to come home. It was over a two-mile walk to school. When I got there, the secretary took one look at me at sent me straight home. Another hike. The next morning, I was rushed into the hospital with a ruptured appendix. Kids died of that condition in those days. I was lucky.

When I reached the ripe old age of sixteen, George planted in my mind the thought of joining the military. I filled out a coupon from one of the national newspapers and sent it off. I did not give it a second thought until a burly Army Sergeant turned up on our doorstep one evening asking for Mr Smith. I automatically assumed he meant my father, but he said, "Mr Dominic Smith." I had never been referred to as mister before in my life.

This was the start of my new life. I spent thirteen and half years serving Queen and Country and loved every second of it. From day one I got three square meals, my own bed, and a set of clothes that had not been worn by my cousin. What can go wrong? At the age of seventeen, I applied to join the Parachute Regiment but failed selection. That took some time to accept, acknowledge and move on. I eventually turned that negative into a positive in my life in the military and more importantly in my police career and undercover life. My military life was a far reach from my young life. I was good at sport, particularly football, I had the gift of the gab, a cheeky Manc. I found military life suited me and I was good at it, and I got 'book smart' to go alongside my 'street smart.'

I married my first wife when we were both young and had two beautiful daughters and now two amazing granddaughters. I reached the rank of Sergeant at the age of twenty-three on merit as opposed to gaining rank via a trade qualification. I became a weapons instructor training recruits. I obtained a Heavy Goods Vehicle, HGV now called LGV, driving licence so I could now legally drive big lorries. Knowledge of weapons and my lorry licence were two skills I was able to put into my future UCO toolbox.

By the time I was thirty I had been divorced and remarried. I continued getting book smart and found myself training the trainer for the Army. This was a completely different role from my trade in the Army. It was during this posting that the police DNA in my system began to stir. My wife, Judy, and I decided that I should apply, and I did. I completed the application, sat the entrance exam, and passed an interview. I had to give the Army one year's notice. The force I joined were relaxed about the delay and I spent the last year of my military career buying a house and completing a resettlement course involving attending seminars and talks on settling back into civilian life. On the day I left the military I took some time to reflect on where I had reached in life: from those simple and difficult beginnings to a successful soldier, homeowner and now a police officer. The only negative, and not one I dwell on, is that some of the lads I ran about with as a kid disowned me for joining the opposition, the police. I adore Manchester but I do not miss it or those that disowned me. I enjoy revisiting and taking my family to my 'Chatsworth Estate'. The streets look smaller, maybe because everyone has a car parked on the road outside their house. Some have removed the hedgerows to create a second car parking space. Those hedgerows that Jimmy once threw me through. I now have a comfortable life and I live in a beautiful part of the world. I thank Manchester for my street education and Manchester United.

Chapter 7

Dominic Session Three

I HAVE NOT MENTIONED my beatings as a child and my parents' behaviour looking for any sympathy or to embarrass my parents in any way. I loved my parents despite all I have said. I wept at their funerals and remembered them on their birthdays and the anniversary of their deaths. My intention is to give you an insight into the building blocks that allowed me to move away from the estate, become a soldier, then a police officer eventually becoming an undercover officer. Working as an undercover officer requires strength of character. My life experiences gathering an array of skills and knowledge combined with the ability to just get on with people, inside and outside the job, as police officers call the police, have greatly helped me in my fifteen years working undercover.

Sometimes the few people in the know have asked me, "What do you need to be an undercover police officer?"

I can tell you I do not know. It is a mixture of many ingredients. You may have a skill or ability that suits a particular role. Like me, you may have circumstances and a background that gives you an edge and the confidence to believe you can do anything but not have a cavalier attitude about it. I had several ingredients in my undercover cake. Those I had gathered as a child, others I picked up in the military and the cream on top when I was a police officer.

Over the years, I have been deployed on many undercover operations. On occasions, I have had to strip naked in front of a criminal to show him I was not wearing a wire. I have been called out as an undercover officer by criminals. To those who ask, "How on earth did he deal with that?" I must say there is no simple answer.

Chapter 8

Dominic Session Four

WHEN I ARRIVED AT my designated Police station, the nick, after training I was assigned to a tutor constable, PC Charlie Thompson. He was a keen weightlifter and had the physique to go with it. I could have done with someone like Charlie around when Jimmy repeatedly threw me into the hedgerows back on the estate. Charlie was a few years younger than me but that made no difference. He had five years of street policing under his belt, what's more, he had a great sense of humour and was outstanding as a cop. Charlie was the Area Beat Officer, ABO, part of the neighbourhood police as we know it today. His patch was a large council estate, so if that's Charlie's arena, it is now mine too. A large council estate, where have we heard that before? Until then I could never quite understand how you could shoot a fish in a barrel. This was home from home for me, and I became a prolific assassin of fish. I was not trigger happy. I did not apply the rule book on every occasion, often using the lawful gift of discretion when dealing with the local population.

On some occasions, I would give verbal advice or a last chance warning. It often depended on the nature of the complaint. For example, if it was a case of minor criminal damage, I would mediate between the two parties and have them resolve their differences without further police involvement. We would attend to domestic disputes, family arguments and fights. I was streets ahead of Charlie in these situations despite his seniority. My method of settling the row would be to take one party out of the house. I would drive them to a friend or family members' house knowing it would be all smiles, kisses and hugs between the two parties the next day. I guess if my parents had taught me anything it was how to deal with domestic violence. There was no point in nicking one of the parties for an overnighter in the cell block, wasting police time and resources.

On a Sunday 2 pm-10 pm shift, we would go around the estate with arrest warrants issued by the courts for defendants who had failed to attend court on a previous date. Charlie and I attended one of the flats to nick a guy called Mo on a failure to attend warrant. Mo was a petty criminal who lived in a top floor flat and was no stranger to the Sunday round-up. On this occasion, Charlie and I entered the flat and found Mo's wife and four children in the lounge in front of their state-of-the-art television. I tugged Charlie's arm and nodded towards the balcony. We both looked towards the balcony, which was about eight feet by three feet, and then back at each other with expressions of total disbelief. Mo's dog was on the balcony, a fully grown Doberman Pinscher, but there was also a mature ropey looking large sheep.

I asked Mo the obvious questions regarding the sheep. He informed me it belonged to his uncle, and he was looking after it for a few days. I knew that was a pack of lies but no way were we nicking him for the sheep rustling. We would have been the laughingstock of the nick and the grief of arranging recovery and identification of the sheep would have been a nightmare. Charlie and I decided to accept Mo's story that it was his uncle's sheep, therefore no theft, no offence. We told Mo we would be back at lunchtime the next day to execute the warrant and the sheep had better be gone. True to our word, we knocked on Mo's door the following day to execute the warrant. We had a quick look around the flat to satisfy ourselves that uncle's sheep had gone. We drove Mo to the local court and before handing him over, he asked for an assurance he'd be back home for his tea. He was.

Over a brew later that day, I said to Charlie, "Do you think we should have checked Mo's freezer?" We both almost choked laughing.

Search warrants were another type of warrant we executed regularly. That involved looking for stolen property or drugs. I enjoyed these intrusions into their lives, strange as that may sound, but only because it reminded me of my youth. We would almost always go through the front door while they were fast asleep tucked up in bed. Depending on the nature of the search we would knock and wait for them to open the door. On other occasions we would let ourselves in using a door opener, a ram, making as much noise as possible to control the occupants and dominate the environment.

Once on a drug search, I found a decent quantity of white powder in the main bedroom. In my professional opinion, it was Colombian marching powder, cocaine. The quantity was sufficient to arrest and charge with the offence of possession with intent to supply. Mr and Mrs, together with their two children were sitting in the lounge under the control and supervision of a colleague. I walked into the lounge with my find. I held up the plastic bag and informed Mr and Mrs that I had found it under their mattress, and I suspected it was cocaine. I cautioned Mr and followed it up with the question, "Is this yours?" He made no reply.

I turned to Mrs, cautioning her and asked the same question and again, no reply. "In that case you are both under arrest on the suspicion of possession with intent to supply a class 'A' drug." As always this was followed up with a further caution which was met with no response.

Mrs then piped up, "You can't do that we've got kids here, that have to get to school."

I came back at her, "Don't worry about that, we will get Social Services in. They'll look after your kids." Some may say that using that tactic is oppressive, I say it is good Old Bill. After an exchange of eye contact and facial expressions between Mr and Mrs, the man of the house admitted it was his and his wife knew nothing about it. A quick reminder he is still under caution, a written note in my pocket notebook, PNB, which I invited him to sign. A confession, the gear (drugs) and one in the bin (cell). Job done. Maybe, a book smart cop that didn't have that streetwise ingredient in their toolbox would have expended more time, effort, and money to obtain, or not, a confession and conviction?

Do not get me wrong when they needed nicking, they got nicked. The net result of dealing with these people in my style of local policing got me a good reputation on the estate and I cultivated a few informants. An informant, a 'snout' or 'grass' is a person, generally a criminal himself or herself, that gives information to the Police on other criminals for their own personal reasons. Those reasons could be revenge, removal of criminal competion, dislike, financial reward and occasionally out of community spirit. In those days the job of 'informant handler' was ninety-nine-point nine per cent conducted by experienced and skilled Detective Constables (DCs) from the Criminal Investigation Department (CID). So not only did I attract the attention of the criminal community on the estate, but I also came to the attention of the CID. I was bestowed with the title 'good thief taker' by my colleagues, detectives, and the CID management. I was so focused on being a top cop I would juggle three or four balls in the air at one time.

I mentioned being an undercover police officer and the balancing act of family life. I'd finished work at around four o'clock one day to pick my daughter up from nursery. I had just got her in my private car when my job phone rang. It was my mate in the office. An informant of mine had called in and needed to see me urgently. I arranged for my mate to call the meeting

on at the local train station car park. I would meet him there
and jump into the plain police car, leaving my young daughter
in my car but always in sight. Shortly after my mate and I met
in the car park, and I jumped from one car to the other. The
snout turned up and jumped into our car. The snout ran out his
information. After I while I noticed that the snout was looking
over my shoulder into the distance. I asked him what was wrong,
thinking he may have noticed someone that had recognised him
and us. He said, "There is a young kid in that car waving at us."
It was my daughter. She still tells that story today.

A system was in place in my force that allowed uniformed officers attachments to CID. With my growing reputation within
CID, it was not long before I was invited on an attachment
which was extended from ten weeks to twenty. During this
prolonged period, I was handed a crime complaint involving a
used car that had been bought on finance from a local dealership. After the first monthly payment had been made no further instalments followed and Mr Tony Wright had disappeared
along with the car. Not the hardest crime to investigate, but this
job eventually took me into the Regional Crime Squad (RCS)
Chief Inspector's (Ch Insp) office and running an international
informant.

I found the car in a different area of the force, still on the
same registration but with a different owner. I recovered the car,
much to the delight of the dealership who had not carried out
all the checks they should have carried out on Mr Tony Wright.
I treated the new owner as an innocent victim knowing he was
well wrapped up in the scam, but it suited me to play him and go
along with his wonky storyline to find Tony. As my investigation into Tony developed, I discovered I was tracking a professional fraudster with South American connections. Tony was
good at conning people and institutions. I fell over mortgage
frauds, credit card fraud, financial fraud. He was Mr Fraud. He
was married to a South American lady. This relationship gave
him access to the cartels and their stock-in-trade of cocaine.

I always seemed to be a couple of weeks behind Tony. In fact, I use to say jokingly, "I wish he'd go on holiday for a couple of weeks so I could catch up with him". One day in the canteen a Detective Sergeant (DS) Vinny Oldman from the RCS approached me and asked if he could sit with me and have a chat. I knew Vinny was a highly respected DS on the RCS. He has been described as a 'Marmite' type character. Well, I love Marmite and I respected and loved Vinny whom I ended up working with later in my career. Vinny began by being almost upfront with me. He asked if I was investigating a guy called Tony Wright and what the investigation was about. We then had a chat which I would describe as shadow boxing all about the subject, Tony. I'll never know if Vinny intentionally gave me a few pointers in that conversation, but I stewed over what he had said and that eventually took me to Tony's front door.

I tracked Tony down to a house in North London with his Colombian wife. I will say right here as soon as we met, I liked him. I did not respect him. He was a likeable cheeky chappy, just like me. He could talk and engage you and take you off the subject if you let him. He had great stories about his life and was tactile with nudges and taps on your arm when he was telling them. We ended up in an interview room at the nick where he admitted the many fraud cases I had against him concluding with a glowing testament to me and my dogged determination tracking him down. Outside the interview room when we were alone doing fingerprints and antecedents, he allowed me to raise my profile as an 'informant handler' to another level.

Tony wanted a deal. He wanted to give me information about drug importations and counterfeit currency on an international scale and he was talking about multi kilos and millions in currency. This was a massive step up for me as a detective and informant handler. Why was Tony giving me this prize? As our professional relationship developed, he told me it was because he liked me. Maybe strangely, I liked him. We had some common ground. Another reason was what is referred to as a 'text'. Every informant, whether fruitful information or not, is entitled to a text to the trial judge at Crown Court. The official name of this text is a 'Piggott text.' A text was produced behind closed doors at court, without my knowledge, and Tony received a suspended sentence.

Tony was given bail from the Magistrates Court, but he was now registered as an informant with me as his handler. He got to work straight away. I received phone calls from him at all times of the day and night asking for a meeting, "Hello, son, it's me, I've got some big stuff for you."

I'll be honest, I loved it. He was the reverse side of the coin to me. The time of the day did not matter, everything was important, had to be acted on here and now. The difference being, he was on one side of the track, and I was on the other.

Tony and I worked on several jobs together and we had a totally professional relationship. On one occasion he requested a meeting at a service station on the M1 motorway. I would always meet him in the company of another officer, normal standard operating procedure (SOP). We met at around six o'clock in the evening over a coffee. He spoke about a parcel of counterfeit Dutch Guilders and produced several samples. This was totally against the rules. To receive the counterfeit notes in the first place he needed permission from the Controller of the Informant handling department. He did not have it. This was a red light for me. I didn't have to worry for long for the following morning Vinny approached me and I was once more invited into the RCS DCIs' office.

Detective Chief Inspector Roger Carter, the DCI, was from a neighbouring force. I did not know him and had never met him, but Vinny was in the office which gave me some security and comfort. I didn't have a clue why I was in there. The DCI did not mess about. The conversation ran something like this:

DCI. "You do not have to admit or deny any of the questions I'm about to ask you. Did you have a meeting with an informant at the M1 service station last night?"

Me. "Yes, I've submitted a contact sheet to my boss this morning."

DCI. "Yes, I know you have. I've got it here" He produced a copy of the contact sheet from a buff-coloured folder. I could see it was a photocopy.

Me. "Am I in the shit here? Should I have a senior officer in here with me?"

DCI. "No way mate. Let me explain. We, me and Vinny, also had a meeting with the same man an hour after you at the same service station. We are obviously handling the same snout (informant) and it cannot be the case either you run him (handle) or we do. I am happy either way"

It was a no brainer for me. I wanted to get onto the RCS. I wanted to work with Vinny, giving up Tony was a small price to pay. The information Tony gave me was not at a local level, it was international, it was what the RCS dealt with and therefore Vinny and his boss were best placed to handle him. I walked away from that meeting knowing that it was the DCI that had written the Piggott text at Tony's Crown Court case, ensuring he did not get a custodial prison term for his multiple frauds. I left the DCIs' office that day and never heard from Tony again until some years later when the phone rang on my desk and the unforgettable voice on the other end said, "Hello, son, it's me."

Once on CID, I gained further experience in investigating, interviewing, giving evidence in Crown Courts and dealing with a more serious level of criminality. One of my greatest strengths was questioning and interviewing suspects. I could pitch my level of conversation or interview with them at a level and a tone that did not wind them up or give the impression I worked to a rigid format with no flexibility in the way the interview would flow. I spoke comfortably in a tone and language that was common to them but at the same time maintained a professional style and approach. I recall conducting several back-to-back interviews with one guy, in the presence of his solicitor (brief), who answered every question with "No comment".

Once the tapes were switched off, he couldn't stop himself from talking to me about football. We had a laugh. All the time I was building up a rapport with him. During one interview after a volley of "no comment" I said, "Okay, then if you do not want to talk about the offence, how about telling us one of those jokes you shared with us when the tapes were off?"

He smiled across the table at me and repeated those immortal words, "No comment".

It was all we could do not to burst out into fits of laughter. Once the tapes had been switched off his brief cleared his throat with a couple of light coughs and said, "I would like to hear what the judge will think of you asking my client to tell a joke during the interview."

Without the need to think about a reply and be confident in my role and the legal process, I immediately responded, "Do you honestly believe that this string of 'no comment' interviews will ever see the inside of a courtroom? Come on."

I was not intimidated by defence solicitors or lawyers in my career. I locked horns with a few over the years in courtrooms up and down the country. They were doing their job and I was doing my job. I can put my hand on my heart and say I have never sent an innocent man to jail, but I have seen guilty men walk free because of a smart brief challenging the police investigation procedures, proportionality, authority levels or a genuine minor mistake by an officer, thus having crucial evidence excluded from the prosecution's case. Their clients get off on a technicality rather than being found not guilty. I often thought about some defence lawyers, have they defended people that they knew were guilty?

Chapter 9

Dominic Session Five

ONCE ON CID, I was focused on joining the Regional Crime Squad (RCS) which later became the National Crime Squad (NCS). Today this organisation is known as the National Crime Agency (NCA). I applied for an interview board to join the RCS at the first opportunity. I only had eight years in the job which was very short service to gain a position on the RCS, but I had a good reputation and bags of confidence. In those days jobs on the RCS already had someone's name on them and the advert and interviews were just a charade. It was always going to be a mate of a mate that got the job. That was the case on my first application. This was my second failure after the disappointment of P Coy (parachute selection) in my military career. However, I had learnt how to turn a negative into a positive and did so on this occasion. Normally after an interview board, you would receive a phone call from one of the interviewing panel to tell you that you have been successful or in my case unsuccessful. I got my phone call from the chair of the board, DCI Roger Carter, Vinny's boss back in the day of Tony, small world! Roger informed me that I had a brilliant interview but unfortunately the job had gone to someone else. I found out later a guy who had a few mates on the RCS had got the job and his name was in the box before it was even advertised. Roger did tell me he was placing a written report on my file highlighting how impressed the panel were with my performance and should I apply again, I should be allowed to attend an interview. I did apply again a few months later and this time I was successful. Maybe my name was in the box this time. But the difference was it was on merit, not nepotism.

Being a member of the Crime Squad was the icing on the cake for me. Not quite the cherry, that was still to come. We were tasked with taking on the top five per cent of the country's Organised Criminal Groups (OCGs) to disrupt and lock them up. We used every conventional and not so conventional police tactic to put these people behind bars, some of whom had the appearance of 'legitimate' successful businessmen. In truth, they were ruthless, violent, career criminals who had no respect for law and order, people, or paying their fair share of taxes. They used violence and the threat of violence as an instrument of terror to achieve their criminal goals and maintain their status within the criminal community. One of the tools we used was deploying undercover police officers (UCOs) into their criminal worlds. This was my introduction to the role and use of UCOs. I was in awe of these men and women and the secret lives they lived. The dangerous situation they placed themselves at the bequest of the Senior Investigating Officer (SIO). The professional manner they conducted themselves at briefings and debriefings was inspiring. They did not turn up at briefings looking like some stereotypical Charlie Big Potatoes talking out the side of their mouths, wearing leather jackets, swearing every other word. They presented themselves without drawing attention. Not in my case, I wanted to know more. I wanted to be part of this exclusive and elite group of detectives. These people did not disturb the environment when they walked into a room, they simply fitted in.

At some point in time after this initial introduction to undercover policing, I applied to be a UCO. Not surprisingly, the process was long and rigorous.

Chapter 10

Dominic Session Six

YOUR POST BACK IN force is not filled when you get seconded to the RCS. That means that they don't move officers around or recruit an additional officer to fill the vacant post. Your home force still manages you, pays you and is responsible for conducting any disciplinary proceedings. You are still one of their officers. In effect, you are loaned to the region to fight cross border crime. There was then and remain forty-three police forces in England and Wales. Northern Ireland and Scotland have their own. That is forty-three Chief Constables together with Deputy Chief Constables (DCCs) and a collection of Assistant Chief Constables (ACCs), not to mention the Heads of Finance and Human Resources. The police service lost twenty-two thousand front line police officers over the current government's tenure. All that prompts me to ask a question: Why are there forty-three Chief Constables and forty-three independent police forces? In my view, we have more chiefs than we have Indians.

A short time after my successful board, I received notification of my start date. Just before that, a DS from my new office contacted me inviting me to meet my new boss, DCI Eamonn O'Donnell. He was a career detective with buckets full of experiences in every avenue of investigation. He was a straight-talking-walking, hard-hitting, no messing individual. He called a spade a spade and when it wasn't, it was a fucking shovel. I was drawn to Eamonn from our first meeting. He had a way of looking at you over his glasses accompanied by a pregnant pause waiting for an answer to his question; waiting to hear if you had an opinion. He would walk into a room and without a word would demand respect. We were in a briefing together with Box (MI5) when somebody from that service gave a load of flannel about an aspect of a job. Eamonn shut him down with a few well-chosen words, his body language and that look over his glasses. My sort of guy. After my long and sometimes dangerous police career, I can count on the fingers of one hand the cops I would follow into battle. Eamonn was one. Outside of that small group, I wouldn't follow any of them around a supermarket.

At our first meeting, DCI Eamonn O'Donnell asked me if I was prepared to join an elite team of officers that were tasked with dismantling and locking up a serious OCG. He added that at that point he couldn't yet say anymore. It was clear, however, I had to commit to the notion and withstand the scrutiny of my police career and discipline record. What was I getting into? I agreed to everything Eamonn asked of me and within a few weeks I was sat at my desk in the RCS office with my two-litre four-door surveillance car in the rear yard and I had Eamonn as my boss. I was loving it.

My time on the RCS and NCS was an amazing period in my life. I worked with some great detectives and some dodgy ones.

From my time on the RCS and NCS, I started to think more about undercover work. Thinking back, I'm not sure where the advert appeared to apply for the role of UCO. Maybe in some national police publication? But I saw it and grabbed the chance with both hands. I wanted to do this stuff. I wanted to beat these crooks at their own game. I wanted to be better than them. I wanted to be that guy that walked into a briefing and the whole room held them in high regard. I really wanted to be an undercover officer.

My first step in an approach to Eamonn as my line manager was to ask him: Would he support my application? Without his endorsement, I was not going anywhere. He sat back in his chair in front of a desk cluttered with papers and files and a copy of a football programme from his beloved team. He looked at me over the top of his glasses, the look I had seen many times before and said in seven words, "You are too nice for that shit."

For a second, I felt that he had pulled the toilet chain inside my heart, then undeterred I smiled at him and thanked him for his kind character reference. I was not going to be put off with his initial reaction and came back at him. We had a frank discussion about the role and my expectations. I felt that I could talk to Eamonn about anything. He was another person that had a great influence on my life. Eamonn had been the SIO on several UC operations, and I truly valued his opinion. But this was something I wanted to do and at the end of the discussion, he agreed to support me. All I had to do was to get the application form, fill it in, and submit it to Eamonn to endorse and approve before sending it off to RCS Head Quarters for a first paper sift.

In due course, the application form arrived in a plain envelope on my desk at the RCS office. That was a positive sign. I'd got past the initial paper sift. Someone was interested in me! I say 'application form,' but it was more like a blank Argos catalogue, and I had to fill the pages with eye-catching words outlining my qualities, experience and desire to be a UCO. They wanted to know everything from my name to my inside leg measurement. More importantly, why?

On the application, I was able to show numerous supporting factors that illustrated my ability, experiences and skills that might be useful as a UCO. I could drive HGVs and I had expert knowledge of firearms. As a result of running informants, particularly Mo, I had extensive knowledge of the South American drug scene, markets, and routes into the UK. I was a mature man that had the gift of the gab. I was highly motivated and wanted the job.

I submitted the completed application to Eamonn who gave me a glowing endorsement. He, in turn, took the application by hand and placed it in the hands of the staff in the RCS undercover unit at HQ. Having run several undercover operations, Eamonn was known and respected by the undercover staff. I learnt later that not only did he give me an outstanding written endorsement, but he also gave me a highly commendable verbal endorsement. Thanks, Eamonn. It was down to me now, pass or fail. I was mentally prepared for either verdict at each step of the process.

After submitting the 'Argos catalogue' application, I continued with my mates, doing my detective work on the RCS against our OCG core nominals. In my own time, I was studying for the next step in the selection process. I read stated cases (law cases that have had a direct impact on undercover policing). I learnt terms such as 'Agent Provocateur' and what that phrase meant. I brushed up on 'direct and indirect questions' and how you avoid falling into the trap of falling foul of Code 'C' of the Police and Criminal Evidence Act (PACE). I studied quantities and prices of drugs, both national and international, road networks, criminal prices of firearms with or without ammunition. I looked at everything they could possibly ask me on the next stage of the path which was an interview board in front of three experienced and senior members of the RCS undercover world. To earn the privilege to gain a seat in front of the board, my application had to pass another paper sift. It was just a waiting game now. There was not a day that passed without me thinking about a decision that was now out of my hands. Every time the phone rang on my desk, my pager sounded or my Nokia mobile phone rang with some irritating ring tone, was this the news, good or bad? I eventually received the good news: "Congratulations you have been given a Regional Board."

On the day of the board a female friend and colleague, Joy, offered to drive me to HQ. I was more than grateful. I don't think my head could have dealt with the traffic and the material filling my brain in preparation for the interview. Before attending I found out who the board members were. An RCS Branch Commander - Chair. Head of the Undercover Unit for my region and a Detective Sergeant (DS) from the Undercover Office who was both a cover officer and an active undercover officer on the National Index. This was the gang of three gladiators waiting to put the Christians who entered the arena to slaughter. Each member had their zone of attack. The chair was very gentle and asked questions about my police and private life. No real curveballs. I was talking about me, and I have never had a problem talking on that subject. The Head of the Undercover Unit drilled into my knowledge on stated cases and laws regarding undercover policing. The DS was the assassin. They had saved the best till last. He took me through a few scenarios. Every time I shut one door; he opened another trap door for me to fall through. The DS was an extremely experienced and talented officer whose reputation preceded him. I got to know him further down the line and discovered those qualities and more particularly his sense of humour.

I left the interview thinking I had blown my chances. I got back in the car with Joy and continually punched the dashboard saying, "I fucked that up" every time I mulled over the questions and my answers in my mind.

I really thought I had given a poor account of myself. Being overly self-critical is one of my character flaws. I'm my own worst enemy and judge, on occasions. Within a few days, my doubts were put to rest when the DS called me to inform me I had successfully passed the board. He congratulated me and we recounted, with humour, some of the trap door scenarios he dragged me through during the interview. No time to sit back and enjoy the moment. The next step was spooky.

It was psychometric testing. There is no research and swotting you can do for this phase of selection. In essence, two trained boffins take you through a series of tests and interviews which they conduct over several days. I was given my day to attend a room in New Scotland Yard (NSY). On arrival, I was directed to a room that was set up in a boardroom layout. There were maybe twenty chairs around the table which were occupied by my competition, men and women from across the forty-three police forces. I certainly felt I was in the company of top cops.

This was the first time I had seen the other officers who had applied for the role. I felt comfortable in their presence and did not see anyone in that room that gave me concern, except for the boffins. The first test was a curveball. We were handed a question booklet. The first page was an example question that the boffins verbally took you through and you had to come up with the solution. This was there to ensure you knew what to do and how to do it. Once everyone had finished the boffins moved around the room checking the answers. I was the only person to get it wrong. Not a good start. After a one-on-one session and the boffins were happy, we were put on a fifteen-minute clock and told to start. The first question was a paragraph of information on three newly built housing estates of properties of different sizes and prices. This was followed by several questions based on different purchasers who had different requirements and available funds. I had to pick out from the information which properties each could afford and that met their requirements. Having completed the first question, I turned the page to read question two. This was about trains, stops and various types of tickets. I had no sooner read the information when one of the boffins told us time was up and we had to put our pens down. I later found out that the booklet contained five questions. I had completed one. A female candidate completed all five questions.

After my day in NSY, I never saw her again. An example of quality over quantity. Further testing involved ticking the box yes or no options. For example, have you ever stolen anything in your life, even a paperclip? 'Yes or No.' If you could fiddle your income tax and get away with it, would you do it? After sheets of these questions, you have a one-on-one interview with the boffins. They ask deep searching questions that obviously give them, together with your test results, a view into your inner self and how you tick. It was a full day at NSY after which the candidates jumped into cars or on trains or made their way to overnight hotel accommodation. I had chosen to travel by train and taxi and joined a few of my competitors for a beer. Most of the conversation was about the process we had all just been through. No one was giving much away or talking about their best top ten jobs. We were in my opinion all top-drawer detectives and strutting around as the great 'I am' was not on the agenda. I engaged in the conversation and banter, but I did not draw unwarranted attention to myself or disturb the group environment. A few pints and a train journey home out of London Euston gave me time to reflect on the day. Still to this day, I cannot work out what selling houses and buying train tickets has to do with undercover policing. I also wonder what the other three questions were about.

Chapter 11

Dominic Session Seven

THE NORMAL WAITING PROCESS followed. My pager, desk phone or mobile would go off and my first thought was the call was from the undercover office. Eventually, the call came inviting me to attend a national interview at a hotel in middle England. I had obviously received a tick in the box from the boffins. This was an interview at a different level. The interviewing panel was made up of the head of the National Crime Squad, the Head of Met Police Undercover Unit and a Detective Inspector (DI), Paul Westly, who had won his spurs as an undercover officer over many years.

The interview progressed much like the regional interview I had successfully negotiated. The first two rounds of questions were quite sedate. It was Paul Westly's job to get me thinking on the spot with crippling scenario questions. At one point I was so wrapped up with his line of questions I found myself leaning forward in my chair towards him tapping the index finger on my right hand on the tips of the fingers on my left hand to reinforce every point in my thought processes. That tactile process was accompanied by me talking through every point forcefully over each particular scenario question. It was not until he accepted my solution to the problem that I realised my body posture was almost inside his personal space. I do not think I did myself any harm. On the contrary, it may have got me across the line. As I said Paul was a legend and arguing a tactic with him is probably not the best course of action if you are looking for a job where you will undoubtedly come across each other in the future.

Another success. I was told the good news after a few days and informed I would be on the next course which was scheduled to start in late February the following year, some months away. In my mind, it was now 'game time.' The additional hard work started now. Not only to get mentally fit but I needed to be match fit. No one ever tells you what to expect on the course or about its content. All people tell you it is based on keeping you under stress and sleep starvation. I'm lucky in that respect I can survive on as little as four hours sleep per night, a bit like Margaret Thatcher. That's where our shared characteristics end. I was relaxed and confident in my knowledge coupled with my experience in life and from my police career that I was ready for the big test. The course is run over two weeks. It starts on a Sunday evening. You work until Friday and have Saturday off. That's a joke, you will see they give you work to do over the weekend. Back on Sunday through to the following Friday.

Before attending you read up on everything undercover, if you know any UCOs you might ask them for tips and advice. The holy rule that everyone that attends the course, pass, or fail, lives by is you never disclose the content or detailed structure of the course to future candidates. Why would you spoil the impactive shock, stress, and unknown content? No one gave me the heads up, and I certainly was not going to do so for anyone. You must arrive with a 'legend'. A legend is a life story and criminality of your alter ego using a pseudonym. For the course, I decided to use the name Doug MacArthur. I prepared my legend with more than just words and was looking forward to running it out when my time came. I had an ace up my sleeve. What is there to worry about? Everything!

I arrived at the designated location early. First one there. Another hang-up from my military days. If the parade was at ten o'clock you were there ready to go by five to ten at the latest. To this day I hate tardiness or being late for an appointment because the person I am attending with is dilly-dallying. This is a constant battleground between me and Sam. Throughout the afternoon the other candidates arrived. I visually and mentally assessed each arrival. I thought that I was going to be in the company of top-drawer cops, the best from over the forty-three police forces. I guess there must have been at least one hundred candidates from the initial request for an application form reduced to the final twelve officers on the course. I would be in the company of giants. I was soon to realise that my background, knowledge, and experience was to give me an advantage over some of my fellow candidates two of whom were females. Ten minutes before the time in the joining instructions to assemble, I made my way from the accommodation block with a couple of the other guys.

We walked into the 'classroom' It was more like a detention room. Nothing was displayed on the walls. It was brightly lit by fluorescent tubes, including one that continuously flickered in tune with the starter motor clicking. Apart from the door into the room, three small narrow windows at ceiling height were the only other break in the room's structure. Not that there was anything to view and allow your mind to wander off the reason for being in this intimidating and hostile environment. An arc of twelve grey plastic chairs was evenly spread out in the centre. I tactically made my way to the chair on the extreme right. I did not want to sit in the middle and be in direct line of sight of whoever was giving instruction. I modestly believe my good looks and air of confidence attracted one of the girls, Tina, better known as 'T,' to take the seat next to me.

As we reached the seats T leaned across a whispered in my ear, "I was heading for that chair, you bastard." So, nothing to do with my magnetic looks and style. A couple of tables with four or five similar chairs randomly placed were in the far corner. The course instructors from the Directing Staff (DS) were taking up three of them. They were huddled over papers and buff-coloured files speaking in low voices, almost in a whisper. They did not break away from their discussion to welcome us let alone acknowledge us entering the room. This tactic of ignoring our existence on the planet created an air of 'them and us.' An uncomfortable atmosphere quickly filled the room. Some of the candidates looked towards each other without breaking their self-imposed vow of silence expressing their unease with facial expressions and raised eyebrows. I sat with my arms crossed across my chest and my legs fully stretched out in front of me. I had given a lot of thought as to what to wear for the initial contact with the directing staff. I did not want to attract attention to myself by dressing up or dressing down. The adage 'Don't disturb the environment' played a part in my choice. Solely for the course, I decided to call myself Doug MacArthur who had a legend in the haulage business. I would dress in casual clothes. A dark polo shirt, black jeans and black Adidas trainers. I hung my dark grey puffer jacket on the back of my chair. I looked along the line of fellow students grading them out of ten on their appearance. Most of them scored high.

Behind us, candidates sat four or five guys. They were seated in the same uncomfortable style of the chair as the candidates. These were observers -middle and senior management detectives. These were the guys that would become the SIOs or team leaders on the future undercover operation and came on a learning exercise to see how these potential future UCOs are trained. One day, they might come and work for them.

I then turned my attention to the huddle of Directing Staff gathered around the tables. I recognised all three from doing my research for the course or from the interviews I had attended. They were all experiences UCOs with mega reputations and egos to match. Paul Hawley sat in the middle of the huddle. He was a real legend in the undercover world. He wrote the book on the then modern National Undercover Training and Assessment Course (NUTAC). If you had not heard of him, you should not be in the room breathing the same air. Go now before you are unceremoniously given the boot. The other two guys were Greg Mann and John Wilson. These three blokes looked like the guy who lived next door or in the line waiting to check-in at the airport. Just normal, regular nine-to-five fellas.

Hawley broke away from the huddle and walked to the centre of the arc. He was in his forties with a good head of dark hair, carrying a bit of weight around his face and gut, dressed in blue jeans and a navy-blue polo shirt. He sported a healthy-looking moustache and spoke in a West Country accent. He stopped a safe distance away from his victims sitting in their grey plastic chairs. For some strange reason, it was at this point I mentally noticed the temperature in the room. It was not too warm or too cold. If you have ever sat in a fast food takeaway such as Micky D's, KFC or Burger King, you will know what I mean. Have you noticed after about twenty, thirty minutes you feel a bit chilly? That's because you are. They set the ambient temperature at a level where it is initially comfortable but after a time it feels just that bit less inviting. This is a great marketing strategy to get you to eat up, rev up and piss off, thereby providing a seat for their next paying customer. I wondered if Hawley had ever been undercover in McDonalds.

His first words were, "Welcome to NUTAC. My name is Paul Hawley and if you don't know who I am you must have been living on the dark side of the moon." The first blast of ego was to be followed by many more from other Directing Staff and role players. Do not misunderstand me, these guys and girls who were acting out their roles had earned the right to have massive egos in the course environment. I learned later in my undercover life when I worked alongside some of them 'the course ego trip' was just that, role-playing. Their role on the course was to intimidate, pressurise and challenge you. Well, I can tell you, in my book it was a ten out of ten start.

Hawley's next few words were, "Who is Tina?"

She raised her arm in the air like a schoolgirl and stated in a strong confident tone, "That's me, staff." Hawley looked in T's direction which brought me into his eye line. That's my plan up the swanee, I thought.

"No need for the staff bollocks in here, Tina. Come out here and let's hear your legend."

Fucking hell, I wasn't expecting a full head-on attack from the word go. Where's all the admin, what to do if the fire alarm goes off, fire exits and all the normal Health and Safety crap. None of that straight into battle. T was the first lamb to the slaughter followed by two more that evening. Not me, thank God. The staff were brutal. They ripped every legend up like toilet paper. No one was good enough. Lesson one, day one, painful.

The course content has probably totally changed since my day and we don't want to spoil it for anyone, do we? I found my level within the group within the first day or so. I realised I had a lot of experience and knowledge which lifted me above the others and when I could I shared these two aspects with my fellow students. The only time I felt I'd screwed up was delivering my legend. It was never going to be an easy ride. My time in front of the staff executioners came on the Sunday evening of week two. In much the same way as T, who together with three other candidates, was no longer with us. Hawley called me out to the front and centre of the group. Turning to face my peers, my heart jumped a beat. Not because I knew I was going to get ragged even if my legend was the best thing since sliced bread. No, I had clocked Mark Peters the guru of all things haulage. He was standing at the back of the room. This guy was a master of the trade. What he didn't know about trucks, routes, loads and regulations was not worth knowing. What I knew compared to him, I could have written on the back of a postage stamp with a pickaxe as a pen. I was fucked, no hiding place. After asking me everything I knew, which didn't take long, about haulage and being a truck driver. He pushed my alter ego on who he was and who he knew and asked for a name he could have a chat with to 'firm things up.' At last, I felt a little bit chuffed with myself. I played the ace from my sleeve. I had jacked up a mate, Bazza, who I had met back in my uniform days. He had since transferred to another force and was already a level one UCO. I had briefed Bazza on my legend and he knew just how to play it should his phone go off with some nosey bastard asking about Doug MacArthur, the lorry driver.

Mark and Bazza had a short exchange over my phone. Bazza played his role like a pro as did Mark. As he passed my phone back to me, Mark asked if Bazza was a six-foot-two mixed-race guy.

"Might be," I said.

Mark continued, "Yeah, I think I might know him, good bloke." He did know Bazza for real from the National UCO Register and had recognised his voice. The uncomfortable, and that's putting it mildly, cross-examination by Mark left me totally deflated. I was waiting for the whisper in my ear, 'Step outside for a mo, Doug.' That was the phrase that signalled the kiss of death on the course and led straight to the car park and the drive home. No soft and fluffy sit-down and a gentle release.

As we were leaving the classroom on the Friday evening of week one to go home one of the directing staff called out to a candidate, "I would think twice about coming back on Sunday evening, mate." Sacked with no comeback or redress to the HR Department. Tough love, indeed.

On Saturday a research project was handed out. It was a topic concerning undercover policing in general or a piece of case law that was important to undercover officers on deployment. The candidates were briefed to research and prepare a presentation to the instructors and fellow candidates in week two of the course. Candidates were called out at random times of the day or night and told to present their subjects. That's an example of how they keep the pressure on. You may have just been given a briefing for a scenario you are about to take part in and getting your head around your role and how to play it, when the instruction to deliver your subject is demanded, "Before we do the next scenario, Doug is going to tell us all about R v Lucas. Over to you Doug." I had researched the case inside out, backwards, forwards and the wrong way round and did a good job.

Week two followed the same path as week one, sleep starvation, pressure, demands, and quick changes in direction with no warning. During that week four further hopefuls received a whisper in their ear. That left four of us, one of the girls and three lads. We saw it through to the end and were rewarded with a number on the National Index and a piss up. I had made it and I was pleased and proud of myself, all that was needed now was that phone call containing the question, "Do you fancy a bit of work?"

Chapter 12

Dominic Session Eight

I SPENT THE NEXT few days recovering and catching up with my family and friends who I had not seen for two weeks straight except for the brief visit home mid-course. I had an inner sense of pride and massive achievement in getting that National Index number and I wanted everyone to know but I couldn't say anything. Yeah, I did share with a couple of close and trusted friends and my then-wife. Judy. The guys and girls I worked with on the National Crime Squad knew my new skill set but it was nothing to sing from the rooftops about. I was still Dom, callsign H9 on the team. Nothing special.

I used some of the time to enhance and build on my legend by adding bits and bobs to my wallet. In my real world, I always carried a black wallet, and still do today. In my legend, my wallet was always brown. A simple little bit of tradecraft that assisted me in perpetuating my alter ego. I created an email account and registered Douglas MacArthur with as many online junk mail companies as I could. I purchased a throwaway, a burner phone from a supermarket megastore somewhere off the M6/M1 motorway miles away from my office or home. OCGs are very resourceful people who by using corrupt police officers, can track down people. Sometimes they might use company employees who want to make a few bob by selling information on where a particular phone was sold and by which outlet. I paid cash and declined the kind offer to sign up for their loyalty card on this occasion as it not only tracks your shopping habits but also tracks you. No thanks. This phone became totally covert. Nothing crossed from Dominic Smith over to Doug. I built up a history on the phone sharing the number with other UCOs and Cover Officers known to me. When Doug's phone rang the name and number that appeared was either a like-minded individual using a pseudonym and throw away phone or some junk company following up on an online search Doug had carried out recently. Doug was growing fast from an embryo to a 'dodgy geezer' with a bit of background.

The official stuff, passport,driving licence, credit card, bank account and an address to tie it all to would be arranged over the coming weeks via my Regional Office. Over the years I developed my alter ego to withstand scrutiny not only from the bad guys and girls, but when needed to obtain services, flights, flats, cars, and hotels around the globe.

Ring, ring. It was Doug's burner phone ringing on the side of the sofa, it was four o'clock on a Sunday afternoon. Excited to answer the call to let the caller know I was on the ball. It could easily have been a payment protection insurance idiot, or an ambulance chasing, no win-no fee claim concerning the accident I had no knowledge of. It was neither. The display showed it was one of the guys from the cover team. I pushed the green phone symbol on the device with enough force to have pushed it straight through the phone and out the other side, I took a deep breath anticipating this was my first job and in a slow matter of fact voice said, "Alright mate, what are you after on a Sunday afternoon?" I was trying not to say 'Yes' before he had asked the anticipated question.

"Are you alright to talk?" was his reply.Those five words became the most asked question of my new career. It was a phrase used by all cover officers and UCOs. It was an indication that the caller wanted to talk privately.

"Yeah, mate sat indoors with the family thinking about tackling the DIY she keeps asking me to get on with,"I said.

Next, I heard, "Do you fancy abit of work?"

Seven little words were music to my ears. I couldn't hold back any longer, before he finished his sentence or told me about the job, I excitingly said, "Yes." The caller then gave me a list of instructions. They included a timetable and a list of locations to collect the other UCOs and get to a briefing in the city. It meant I had to be on the road by five the following morning. I had to get to the office; master the alarm system; collect a covert vehicle; drive to three further locations to collect the other UCOs, and then get to the briefing location all before nine o'clock.

I completed my tasks and had everyone in the right place by the right time. The briefing was delivered bythe SIO, and the cover officer conveyed how the UCOs were going to carry out the deployment. This had already been pre-agreed, so it was more of a formality.My three fellow UCOs were given active roles dealing with the money, testing the gear (drugs), and one acting as the leader of our gang. My job was to drivethe car; drop them off and wait around the corner. I didn't even see a bad man let alone speak to one. I didn't care because I'd been blooded; I'd been across the pavement; I'd done my first job. All I had to do after completing my notes was revert to the taxi driver role and get my fellow warriors home and collect my car from the office. This was the first of many jobs I deployed on over the next fifteen years. By the end of my undercover tenure, I was the guy the new boy came and picked up after he'd been chased ragged before getting to me.

There is a pecking order in the undercover policing world and quite rightly so. The more jobs you do the greater amount of experience and knowledge you gain. Early in my undercover career, I was drafted into a long-term international drug buy. Together with another UCO, it was planned for me to sit in a hotel room in New York, USA, along with a couple of the bad guys while the deal went down in North London.We were paying for the parcel (drugs) in US dollars and the parcel was being delivered in London. It was going to be controlled over phones in veiled speech. Beforehand, I attended a meeting with the other UCOs, the SIO and a few of his operational team. But before we entered the meeting room, I recognised one of the other UCOs as a role player from my undercover course. He asked if I was Dom. I confirmed I was and shook his hand. He then burst my bubble when he said, "You think you're going to New York. Not now, you are on the other half of the job in London and I'm in New York. You okay with that?"

I wasn't going to complain, "Yeah, no worries, buddy. I'm just pleased to be involved with you guys." That was a bit of a tummy rubbing exercise on my behalf, which is never a bad thing. The job fell out of bed (was abandoned) owing to too many moving parts.

Over the years I attended a firearms course with Special Forces handling every known firearm you can imagine. Drugs courses were dealing with the different drugs and street testing techniques designed to prevent getting ripped off when buying a parcel of heroin. I ended up driving HGVs in the UK and Europe doing real haulage; picking up and tipping loads so I could talk the talk and walk the walk when purporting to be a real lorry driver. I attended courses dealing with contract killing, kidnapping and extortion and sailing yachts. You never knew when some of this knowledge would prove to be useful. I took every opportunity to enhance my education around OCGs and improve my skill set.

Chapter 13

Paul Nuemann

"THERE YOU HAVE IT. Straight from the horse's mouth, so to speak. So, what makes them tick?" Paul Nuemann said.

Someone called out, "Determination."

"Determined to do what?"

"Be the best UCO in the elite. The elite of the elite."

Another called out, "Confidence. In their own abilities and their cover officers and operational teams including their SIOs."

Then someone else, "Family bonds. Not only their own and extended family but also the family of undercover officers... the brother or sisterhood of UCOs."

A woman at the back chirped up, "Discipline, by that I suppose I mean self-discipline, integrity, resoluteness."

Paul Neumann raised his hand in a silencing gesture before he next spoke, "Clearly you all have a handle on what made these two officers remarkably successful. I wouldn't disagree with any of those attributes you called out. It is neither possible nor desirable to carry out a lobotomy on Mr and Mrs Smith to see if there are any physiological reasons for their suitability to these demanding roles..." a polite laugh was heard around the room before Neumann continued, "but what is possible, indeed imperative, is their psychological profiles are transformed into benchmarks for the future selection and training of undercover officers."

"Mr Edwards, perhaps you are better placed to answer my question?" ACC Tony Williams of the Merseyside Police said.

"I'll do my best, Tony, what is it?" ACC Edwards said.

ACC Tony Williams of the Merseyside Police was an old school career detective who had once worked undercover on the Merseyside Undercover Unit. He paused before he said, "Do you or Mister Neumann think developing profiles for the desired qualities in future undercover offices may become redundant in not too many years ahead?"

ACC Edwards said, "Interesting question, what do you think?"

Williams said without hesitation, "It may. We are all aware the new forms of recruiting police officers will be rolled out in the next few years. That involves ensuring all new police officers are degree-educated including the new policing degree. It concerns me that the route into undercover policing for former services personnel will effectively be removed. No more Dominic Smiths."

"Good point, Tony, and noted. I will make sure that goes into the final recommendations. There may be a case for direct entry into covert policing for suitable ex-services personnel," Edwards said.

Blunt as always, Williams had the last word, "That will never happen. It's too elitist or so the government will say. You know elitism has always been discouraged in the British police service."

Author's Note

Do you wonder what Operation Candle was all about? 'Undercover Legends' is planned as a series featuring not only Dom and Sam but other undercover officers as well as some villains of the piece.

Other than this first book, Meet Mr and Mrss Smith, the second book in the series is titled *Undercover Legends: The Real Mr and Mrs Smith* and is now as an eBook, paperback and audiobook. Operation Candle is mentioned frequently in that book. The third book in the series will be *Operation Candle: Undercover Legends*.

Operation Candle was a real and unique undercover operation set up to counter an intelligence black hole in a fictional town that could be Birmingham, Burnley or Bristol. There was an area of the town known to be a hive of activity populated by an organised crime group. There were no informants on the ground. These criminals thought they were fireproof and would never be caught.

Dom, Sam and a UCO called Phil, devised a plan to embed themselves in the community with Sam posing as a business-woman operating online lingerie, designer handbags and clothing business. Phil's cover story was about an online business selling sports gear. With the help of a police technical support department, they got to work building websites, arranging covert personal and business bank accounts, credit cards, driving licences and passports.

At the outset, Dom said to Phil and Sam, "You never know there could be some air miles in this job."

Little did he know, he was right. Operation Candle was an amazing 'bit of work.'

About the Author

DAVID LE COURAGEUX IS a pen name used by a writing team in the Undercover Legends series. Stephen Bentley is a member of that team. He is a former British police Detective Sergeant, pioneering Operation Julie undercover detective, and barrister. He now writes in the true crime and crime fiction genres and contributes occasionally to Huffington Post UK on undercover policing, and mental health issues.

He is possibly best known for his bestselling Operation Julie memoir and as co-author of *Operation George: A Gripping True Crime Story of an Audacious Undercover Sting*.

His Operation Julie book has been optioned and is in development as an 8-part TV series in addition to that huge and unique police operation being pitched to broadcasters as a documentary. He is pleased that *Operation George* has also been optioned for the TV screen.

Stephen is a member of the UK's Society of Authors and the Crime Writers' Association.

Now a multi-genre author, Stephen also writes cozy mysteries in the pen name of KJ Cornwall.

You can listen to Stephen talking about his Operation Julie undercover days on the BBC Radio 4 Life Changing programme/podcast available 24/7 worldwide on BBC Sounds. And on the same platform, he also contributes to Acid Dream: The Great LSD Plot.

Sign up to the mailing list for news of books by Stephen here[1]
.

---

1. Newsletterhttps://stephenbentley.eo.page/rz1db

Also By

You can find all books written by Stephen Bentley and his pen names including KJ Cornwall using the Booklinker images below or viewing here.

You can also buy his books direct here.

KJ Cornwall Books2Read page is here. Stephen Bentley Books2Read page is here.

Visit the links by using the QR codes below for more details:

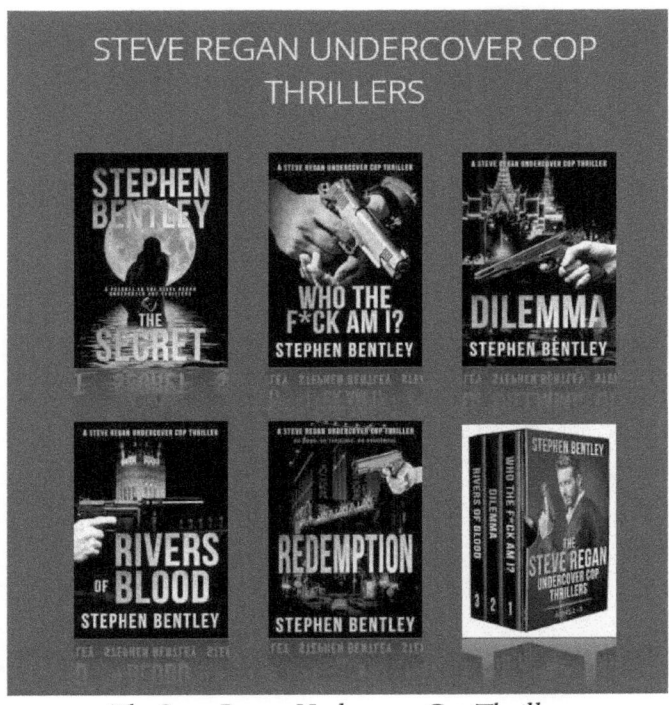

The Steve Regan Undercover Cop Thrillers

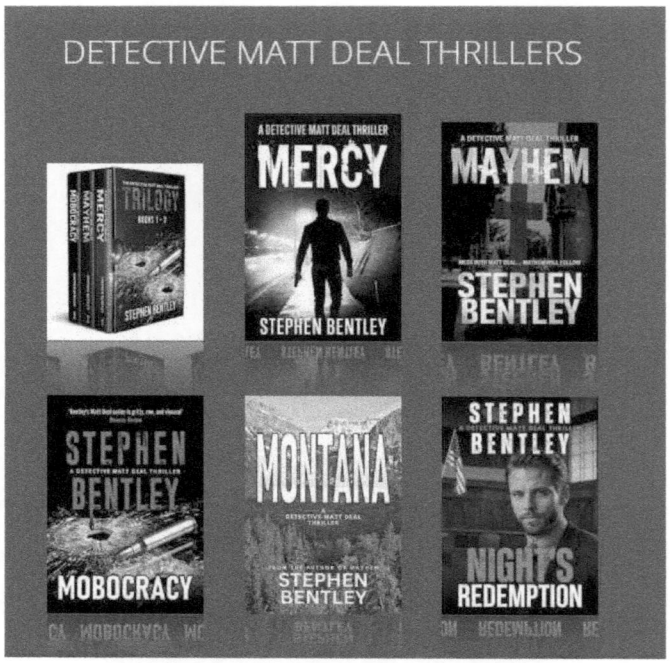

The Detective Matt Deal Thrillers

Bestselling True Crime

If you prefer to use QR codes you can find out more about all books written by KJ Cornwall and sign up for the mailing list by scanning the QR code below.

Similarly, you can find full details of true crime books and hard boiled thrillers written by Stephen Bentley by scanning the QR code below.

www.ingramcontent.com/pod-product-compliance
Ingram Content Group UK Ltd.
Pitfield, Milton Keynes, MK11 3LW, UK
UKHW040622240925
8053UKWH00038B/350